I Used to
Know That

CIVIL WAR

I Used to Know That

CIVIL WAR

stuff you forgot
from school

FRED DuBOSE

Reader's
Digest

The Reader's Digest Association, Inc.
New York, NY

U.S. Project Editor: Kim Casey
Project Designer: Elizabeth Tunnicliffe
Copy Editor: Barbara Booth
Indexer: Nan Badgett
Senior Art Director: George McKeon
Executive Editor, Trade Publishing: Dolores York
Manufacturing Manager: Elizabeth Dinda
Associate Publisher, Trade Publishing: Rosanne McManus
President and Publisher, Trade Publishing: Harold Clarke

Library of Congress Cataloging-in-Publication Data
DuBose, Fred.
   I used to know that : Civil War : stuff you forgot from school / Fred DuBose.
   p. cm. -- (I used to know that)
Includes index.
ISBN 978-1-60652-244-8
   1. United States--History--Civil War, 1861-1865. I. Title. II. Title: Civil War.
   E468.D825 2011
   973.7--dc22

                              2010051830

For more Reader's Digest products and information, visit our website:
          www.rd.com (in the United States)

Printed in the United States of America

1 3 5 7 9 10 8 6 4 2

Acknowledgments

Special thanks go to Richard Bailey, whose studious research and advice proved
invaluable as this book took shape. The contributions of writers Martha Hailey,
Bruce Kauffman, and David Diefendorf are also greatly appreciated. The librar-
ians at the New York Public Library deserve a grateful nod as well—as do the
following people, organizations, and institutions:

• Curt Anders, Sarah Arnold, Jim Buie, Dr. Victoria E. Bynum, Nell Campbell,
Scott Gampfer, Annette Haldeman, Hari Jones, Robert Keathley, Alfred Kennedy,
Patricia Keats, Deb King, Phillip Mitchell, Patricia Murphy, Cassandra Reagor,
Donna Schmidt, Mark Thomas, Jim Waecter, and Carl Westmoreland

• African-American Civil War Museum, Alexandria (New Hampshire) Historical
Society, Ball County (Virginia) Historical Society, Cincinnati History Museum,
General Lew Wallace Study and Museum, Hildene Estate, Maryland Historical
Society, Maryland Legislative Reference Library, Museum of the Soldier, National
Underground Railroad Freedom Center, and the Society of California Pioneers

Page 2: Engineers of the 8th N.Y. State Militia, 1861

Contents

———⟨◉⟩———

The Antebellum Period, 1800–1860

10

For decades America's most divisive bone of contention—the slave system—gradually disappeared in the North but remained entrenched in the South. This chapter looks at key abolitionists (all, at first, reviled by society at large); philanthropists who furthered the cause; journalists and authors who changed millions of minds; politicians whose well-meaning legislation actually spurred the march toward Civil War; and free blacks and fugitive slaves who could vote only with their words or their feet.

The War between the States, 1860–1865

62

In 1860 the lightning-bolt election of Abraham Lincoln ignited the secession of slave states and the nation's costliest war by far. This chapter takes you to the key battles fought in the three main theaters of war and introduces you to the Civil War's cast of characters—the commanders-in-chief, officers, rank and file; the spies, guerillas, secret sympathizers, and renegades; and the medical corps and ordinary citizens who cared for the wounded and dying.

The Reconstruction Era, 1865–1877

150

Discord continued between northerners and southerners after the end of the war—the 20-year period of Reconstruction. This chapter includes speculation on the course history might have taken if Lincoln had not been assassinated; the South-loathing Radical Republicans who went after his successor Andrew Johnson with a vengeance; legislative amendments that gave equal rights to former slaves in theory but not in practice; and the truth about those so-called carpetbaggers.

Introduction
The Road to War

Flirtation with secession is as old as the United States itself. New York anti-Federalists almost refused to ratify the Constitution. A handful of Federalist objectors to the War of 1812 argued for the secession of New England. South Carolina declared federal tariffs increasing the cost of imported goods null and void with an 1832 ordinance, then passed a law authorizing a state military force—a bold stand for "states' rights."

Despite such threats, our earliest statesmen could hardly have imagined a day when the sons of the North and South would battle to the death for four long years. How could such a conflict have come to pass?

Distant Worlds Rice, indigo, and cotton were the South's cash crops from the colonial days on. Cotton production increased sevenfold between 1830 and 1850, and the slavery on which it relied became more and more entrenched.

At the same time, sectionalism—excessive devotion to regional interests—tightened its grip. People of the sparsely industrialized South took pride in their suspicion of the federal government, the gentility of the planter class, the slow pace of life, and even their paternalism toward the 40 percent of the population in bondage.

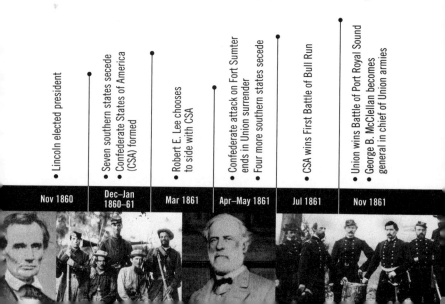

- Lincoln elected president

- Seven southern states secede
- Confederate States of America (CSA) formed

- Robert E. Lee chooses to side with CSA

- Confederate attack on Fort Sumter ends in Union surrender
- Four more southern states secede

- CSA wins First Battle of Bull Run

- Union wins Battle of Port Royal Sound
- George B. McClellan becomes general in chief of Union armies

| Nov 1860 | Dec–Jan 1860–61 | Mar 1861 | Apr–May 1861 | Jul 1861 | Nov 1861 |

As farmland became exhausted, planters aimed to move on to new territories and take slavery with them. Politically, "slave power" gave Southerners congressional influence beyond their numbers, and legislative compromises, which beginning with the Missouri Compromise of 1820, sought to maintain the balance of power between northern and southern states.

The North was an industrial powerhouse. Its vestiges of slavery disappeared in the 1820s, and increasing urbanization and diversity became the new normal above the Mason-Dixon Line. "Free Soil, Free Labor, Free Men" was a byword, but many Northerners feared the prospect of competing with freed blacks for jobs.

Whether slavery would die a natural death over time or spread throughout a nation poised to conquer the world was the burning question.

Politics and Religion Naturally, not all Southerners were pro-slavery, and not all Northerners were antislavery. But it was majority opinion that mattered. At mid-century, political parties were molded from factions of old ones, and the Republican Party emerged as the voice of those who wanted to halt the expanse of slavery to territories soon to be annexed as states. The Democratic Party would split over the issue.

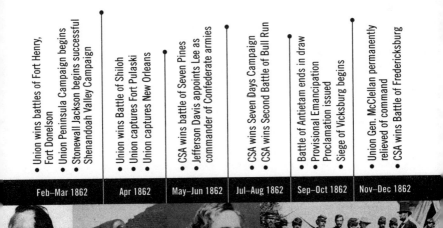

| Feb–Mar 1862 | Apr 1862 | May–Jun 1862 | Jul–Aug 1862 | Sep–Oct 1862 | Nov–Dec 1862 |

Feb–Mar 1862
- Union wins battles of Fort Henry, Fort Donelson
- Union Peninsula Campaign begins
- Stonewall Jackson begins successful Shenandoah Valley Campaign

Apr 1862
- Union wins Battle of Shiloh
- Union captures Fort Pulaski
- Union captures New Orleans

May–Jun 1862
- CSA wins battle of Seven Pines
- Jefferson Davis appoints Lee as commander of Confederate armies

Jul–Aug 1862
- CSA wins Seven Days Campaign
- CSA wins Second Battle of Bull Run

Sep–Oct 1862
- Battle of Antietam ends in draw
- Provisional Emancipation Proclamation issued
- Siege of Vicksburg begins

Nov–Dec 1862
- Union Gen. McClellan permanently relieved of command
- CSA wins Battle of Fredericksburg

Throwing morality and civil rights into the mix were social reforms born of the so-called Second Great Awakening—the Protestant revivalist crusade that swept the nation in the early 1800s. Activists in the North and South alike launched temperance, women's suffrage, and abolition movements, and the abolitionists set off the noisiest alarms.

A Quadruple Whammy In the 1850s four key events—three legislative and one literary—inched the nation toward disunion.

★ **Compromise of 1850** This act was a payoff to the South for its support of the admission of California as a free (nonslave) state and the end of slave trading in Washington, D.C. The poison pill within was the Fugitive Slave Law—so grievous it tipped on-the-fence Northerners to the antislavery side and increased traffic on the Underground Railroad.

★ **Publication of *Uncle Tom's Cabin*** Harriet Beecher Stowe's 1852 novel depicting the human costs of slavery heightened antislavery sentiment in the North and outraged the slaveholding South.

★ **Kansas–Nebraska Act of 1854** This act stipulated that a vote by citizens of a territory would determine its free-state or slave—state status. Violence soon

• Emancipation Proclamation takes effect
• Black soldiers join Union Army
• CSA wins Battle of Chancellorsville
• Union wins Battle of Gettysburg
• Union wins eight-months-long siege of Vicksburg
• CSA wins Battle of Chickamauga
• Lincoln delivers Gettysburg Address
• Union wins Battle of Chattanooga
• Ulysses S. Grant takes command of all Union armies
• Grant's five-week Overland Campaign ends with defeat at Cold Harbor

| Jan 1863 | May–Jun 1863 | Jul–Aug 1863 | Sep–Dec 1863 | Mar 1864 | May–Jun 1864 |

erupted in Kansas as free-staters and proslavery guerrillas fought over its fate.

★ **Dred Scott Decision** The Supreme Court's 1857 ruling in *Scott vs. Sandford* not only declared the Missouri Compromise unconstitutional (stripping Congress's power to ban slavery in new territories) but also made it impossible for even free blacks with slave ancestry to become citizens.

The Split One blood-soaked fighter in Kansas was John Brown, who hatched a plot to start a slave rebellion and, in 1859, attacked the federal arsenal in Harpers Ferry, Virginia. After Brown's trial and execution, the national fever rose as adversaries celebrated his martyrdom or decried his wild-eyed fanaticism.

It wasn't Brown who ignited the spark that flamed into Civil War. It was the November 1860 election of Abraham Lincoln (not a die-hard abolitionist, but dead set against slavery's spread) and the subsequent secession of seven states.

If it weren't for slavery, sectional differences might have been resolved in the political arena. As it was, the men fondly or derisively called Rebels, Johnny Rebs, graycoats, and seceshes were about to battle Yankees, Billy Yanks, and bluecoats in the gravest crisis ever to face the nation.

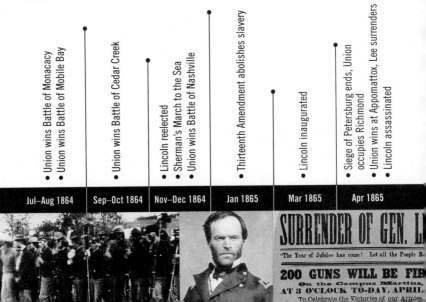

THE
ANTEBELLUM
PERIOD

1800–1860

During the Revolutionary War, Vermont was the only state that drew up a constitution prohibiting slavery. With the war won and the new nation rapidly expanding westward, the question of whether states would be free states or slave states would become no small matter of concern. Abolitionism slowly gained ground as one of the social reforms of the early nineteenth century, and by no means only in the North. Then, in mid-century, legislative compromises to keep a balance between free states and slave states heightened the likelihood of war.

This chapter focuses on the leading figures who emerged and the events that shaped their actions. Whether white or black, statesmen and activists took some very different approaches to the political and moral issues of the time.

The U.S. Capitol dome under construction, 1860

POLITICIANS PRESENT AND FUTURE

Whether they led by design or by destiny, five elected officials
and two military leaders who came of age in the antebellum
years faced winds of discontent blowing over the
whole of the North and South.

―――――《◎》―――――

Bound for Power

Political movers and shakers who rose to prominence included
a gangly lawyer from Illinois, a planter's son from Mississippi, a
president who went to war to expand territorial boundaries, and
two southern slaveholders.

☛ TWO BIRTHS IN KENTUCKY

Abraham Lincoln came into the world on a farm near Hodgen-
ville, Kentucky, on February 12, 1809, less than nine months
after Jefferson Davis was born about a hundred miles away in
Fairview. Lincoln had sporadic schooling as a boy and began to
educate himself at age 15. Davis graduated from military school,
college, and West Point. From April 1861 to April 1865, these
two men would match wits as commanders in chief of armies
battling to save or divide the Union.

☛ LINCOLN'S UPWARD CURVE

Thomas Lincoln, the father of the man who would one day issue
the Emancipation Proclamation, took his family to an Indiana
farm in 1816 and later to Illinois. In 1831 his 22-year-old son
Abraham moved to the bustling village of New Salem, 20 miles
upriver from the state capital of Springfield. It was here he consumed books on history, law, philosophy, and grammar in great

gulps. His skill at selling dry goods and any other commercial endeavor, his ingenuity, and his way with words did not go unnoticed. In particular, Lincoln's witty yet rock-solid arguments at the local debating society made many in New Salem believe he was bound for greater things.

It was local admirers who urged Lincoln to run for the Illinois state legislature. He announced his candidacy in spring 1832 and then ran a campaign showcasing both his grasp of local issues and his humble origins. He lost, but the public was given its first taste of the qualities that would one day put Abraham Lincoln in the White House. In the interim he would cut his national-service teeth with a term in the U.S. House of Representatives (below).

Honest Abe

Legend holds that Lincoln the store clerk came to be known as Honest Abe for his alleged miles-long walks to repay an overcharge or return the balance for an undercharge. In truth, it was Lincoln the lawyer's unwavering honesty and refusal to overcharge clients that earned him the nickname. Such character traits may explain in part how Lincoln achieved public office five times between 1834 and 1847—four terms in the Illinois state legislature and once in the U.S. House of Representatives (1847–1849).

Lincoln and the Law Just as his debates in New Salem would hone Abraham Lincoln's skills as a lawyer, his law practice in Springfield—where he moved in 1837—would sharpen his political savvy. His earnings, however, were merely adequate. So like many lawyers, he supplemented his income by traveling around the state with circuit judges. He joined the court caravan either in the saddle—his horse was named Old Tom—or a buggy. And decent room and board for Lincoln and his law partner—James Herndon, his third—was catch as catch can. To Lincoln's regret, traveling the circuit meant leaving his wife, Mary, whom he had married in 1842, and his four sons for at least three months a year.

Introducing "The Railsplitter" Two events went a long way toward bringing Lincoln to national attention:

★ In 1858 he challenged Illinois senator Stephen A. Douglas for his seat—and if he lost the battle, he won the war. In a series of seven debates with Douglas, Lincoln's masterful arguments for excluding slavery from new territories not only established his antislavery credentials but also were printed and distributed for all to see.

★ His 1860 speech at Cooper Union (New York City's new tuition-free university), with the same antispread of slavery bent, was the talk of the national press.

The Railsplitter in his presidential-candidate garb

Before the Republican National Convention of 1860 opened in Chicago, Illinois, legislators chose former congressman Lincoln as their favorite son for the presidency. His supporters worked behind the scenes to spring a surprise, and one brilliant stroke came from an operative who thought Lincoln's "Honest Abe" name was too bland.

A trip out to the old Lincoln family farm yielded two appropriately rustic rails from a split-rail fence. Their labels described Lincoln as "The Rail Candidate" and claimed the rails came from a log split by Lincoln and his uncle. The gambit succeeded, and the future president was off and running.

☛ JEFFERSON DAVIS: West Point and Beyond

The youngest of Samuel and Jane Davis's 10 children, Jefferson Finis Davis, was born in Kentucky and grew up on the family's cotton plantation in Mississippi. By the time he entered West Point, he was clearly a rebel. His academic record was average, but he excelled at earning demerits for breaking curfew, frequenting a local source of hard liquor, and generally disregarding the rules. He was once court-martialed for his participation in a student riot, fueled by alcoholic eggnog, and barely avoided expulsion.

Davis's Service to the Union His high jinks behind him, Davis became an excellent soldier as colonel of the 1st Mississippi Rifles regiment and, later, a two-term senator (1847–1851, 1857–1861).

It was in the Mexican War (page 17), during the Battle of Buena Vista, that Col. Jefferson Davis issued his "Stand fast, Mississippians!" battle cry to his militiamen. The regiment under Davis, who was wounded but stayed in the fight, gained international fame for its daring and successful assault on the powerful forces of Mexican General Santa Anna. But this would hardly be Davis's only service to the U.S. military.

From Camels to Cabinet Appointed secretary of war by President Franklin Pierce in 1853, Davis pushed for major expansions of the army, including the addition of new mounted units; insisted that the infantry be equipped with more accurate and reliable weapons; and revised infantry tactics with more emphasis on skirmishing. He also retained some of the fanciful nature of his West Point days, championing the importing of camels for military use in the arid Southwest (a project that came to fruition but would be canceled by the Union Army in 1863).

Four years at the helm of the War Department told Davis just how ill prepared the South was for military conflict. On his return to the Senate in 1857, he was determined to prevent Southern secession.

☞ HENRY CLAY: The Great Compromiser

Kentucky senator Henry Clay, a slaveholder who built a thriving Kentucky plantation outside Lexington, adamantly opposed the idea of Manifest Destiny, a term coined by writer John O'Sullivan to glorify the mission of (white) America to expand its territory continent-wide. He was also the man who would be president but never was. He ran five times as a Whig Party candidate, and probably would have beaten Democrat James K. Polk in 1840 if Liberty Party founder James G. Birney had not won some 62,000 votes. (Polk and his fellow Democrats wielded the Manifest Destiny slogan to justify the Mexican War.) Yet as three-time Speaker of the House—he was first elected at age 34—Clay turned the speakership into the second most powerful position in government.

Major Acts Clay brokered the free state–slave state compromises of 1820 and 1850 (page 18). But the label he earned—the Great Compromiser—may have grown not only from these seemingly pragmatic but flawed bills but also from the geniality and diplomacy that made him one of nation's favorite politicians.

☞ JAMES K. POLK: Presidential Campaign Pushes Debate into Slavery High Gear

James K. Polk, a Jeffersonian Democrat yet a protégé of Andrew Jackson (page 60), ran his successful 1844 presidential campaign largely on the immediate annexation of the Republic of Texas. Disputes over ownership and boundaries had continued since Texas declared its independence from Mexico in 1836 and then defeated the Mexican Army. Yet Mexico refused to accept Texas as sovereign.

The Mexican War

As President Polk looked for excuses to send troops to Texas, he eyed additional Mexican and British possessions in the West. War was declared on May 13, 1846, and with it came battles in Congress over slavery. In August, Pennsylvania congress-

A cartoon lampoons the rawness of Mexican War recruits.

man David Wilmot introduced the Wilmot Proviso, a bill rider that would ban slavery in territory acquired in the war. Debates reached a fever pitch, and the bill did not pass in the Senate.

When Polk's war ended in victory in September 1847, the Treaty of Guadalupe Hidalgo provided vast western territories from which states from Oregon to New Mexico would be carved. Along with the Wilmot Proviso debates, this expansion elevated slavery to the nation's dominant political issue until the Civil War.

☛ JOHN C. CALHOUN: The Cast-Iron Man

Like Henry Clay, South Carolina senator John C. Calhoun backed the Fugitive Slave Act (pages 18, 55). More than a decade before its passage in 1850, he delivered his famous "Slavery: A Positive Good" speech on the senate floor. "Never before has

Pivotal Legislation

No force affected popular opinion and the course of abolition-ism more than laws regarding slavery. Two compromises put forth by Henry Clay only furthered the march toward war.

Missouri Compromise of 1820

In 1819 the equal balance of free and slave states—11 each—was threatened when the Missouri Territory sought annexation. Because most of Missouri's citizens were from the South and many held slaves, Northerners in Congress introduced an amendment to prohibit further slavery there. The bill passed in the House but failed in the Senate.

The issue was resolved with a two-part compromise. The northern part of Massachusetts became Maine and was admitted to the Union as a free state. At the same time, Missouri was admitted as a slave state, thereby maintaining the free state–slave state balance.

In addition, an imaginary line was drawn at 36° north latitude, and any territory lying north of the line would be free. Yet fugitive slaves could be lawfully reclaimed even in free territories.

Compromise of 1850

Clay first proposed this legislation when territories won in the Mexican war were annexed. The Compromise of 1850 accommodated various political interests and had five stipulations:

★ California would be admitted as a free, not slave, state.

★ Citizens of New Mexico and Utah would be allowed to resolve the slavery issue by popular vote.

★ Texas was forbidden to expand into New Mexico in exchange for the government's payment of its U.S. debts.

★ The slave trade was abolished in Washington, D.C., though slavery itself was not.

★ An exceptionally harsh Fugitive Slave Act became law.

the black race of Central Africa, from the dawn of history to the present day," he asserted at one point, "attained a condition so civilized and so improved, not only physically, but morally and intellectually." The fact is, the majority of Americans of the 1830s sympathized with this notion—even people who saw slavery as a necessary evil and, in some cases, those who called for its immediate end.

The son of a prosperous South Carolina slaveholder, Calhoun served as U.S. representative, secretary of war under James Monroe, vice president under John Quincy Adams, and secretary of state under John Tyler. But it was his 14 years in the senate that earned him the name "Cast-Iron Man," a reference to his determined defense of his causes. In time Calhoun evolved from a nationalist and opponent of protective tariffs to a staunch supporter of free trade, state's rights, and limited government.

Generals in the Making

The men would go head-to-head in the Civil War—General in Chief Ulysses S. Grant of the Union Army and his southern counterpart, Robert Edward Lee—both overcame less-than-perfect childhoods.

☛ H. ULYSSES GRANT: A Bumpy Road

As a boy, Hiram Ulysses Grant was small in build, rather aloof, and not one to break into smiles. It would have been hard to take pleasure in the work he did with his father, who tanned hides for a living on a farm outside Georgetown, Ohio. Yet Lyss, as he was called, came alive when tending and breaking horses on the Grant farm.

School to Service In 1839 Grant entered West Point. He was a mediocre student, but no other cadet could touch his skills as a horseman. After he graduated, those skills would serve him well when he was assigned to the Fourth U.S. Infantry in Missouri. The Mexican War took Grant to Texas and Mexico, where as a lieutenant he was cited twice for bravery. He also came away with an understanding of the logistics of war.

Grant's Down Time The next dozen odd years would lead Grant to marriage and four children but also to failed jobs, financial ruin, and excessive drinking. In 1860 he moved his family to Galena, Illinois, where he languished as a clerk in his father's leather store. Before long, war would break out with the Confederate attack on Fort Sumter. So in July 1861 Grant was back in uniform, where—as time would tell—he had always belonged.

General Grant with his daughter Nellie, sons Jesse and Frederick, wife Julia, and son Ulysses junior

"S" Stands for Nothing

When H. Ulysses Grant entered West Point, he was in for a surprise. Thomas L. Hamer, the Ohio congressman who had nominated him at the request of Grant's father, Jesse, had been hazy on the young man's full name. He thought Grant's mother's maiden name was a good bet, and so he wrote Ulysses *Simpson* Grant on the application—and once on the record, it stayed. Grant later adopted the name's initial but insisted it "stands for nothing."

☛ ROBERT E. LEE: A Lesson Learned

Robert E. Lee came from one of Virginia's most notable families (two Lees signed the Declaration of Independence). He also grew up with few of the privileges of wealth and power. His father, Henry ("Light Horse Harry") Lee III, had been a hero of the Revolutionary War and later served as governor of Virginia and a U.S. senator. But Henry Lee's real passion was speculative investments. By the time Robert was three, his father was so deeply in debt that everything he and his wife owned had been cashed in or sold, and the Lees were reduced to genteel poverty.

Life without Father In 1813 six-year-old Robert saw his father for the last time. Leaving the family to fend for themselves, Henry fled to Barbados to escape his creditors and avoid jail. He died unexpectedly while trying to return home.

Robert was devoted to his mother, Ann Carter Lee, but never spoke much about his childhood or his father. Perhaps the reckless and mostly absent Henry provided an object lesson in what *not* to be. As biographer Douglas Southall Freeman observed, "Self-denial and self-control were the supreme rule of life" and "the basis of [Lee's] code of honor."

THE ABOLITIONISTS

Abolitionists ran the gamut in beliefs, level of intensity, and skin color. They were also heirs of the founders of the earliest antislavery groups—one being the Society for the Relief of Free Negroes Unlawfully Held in Bondage, which began meeting in Ben Franklin's Philadelphia in 1775.

Leading Lights

Among the leading antislavery activists were a fiery journalist, a fugitive slave, two highly successful free blacks, and a former slaveholder from the South.

☛ WILLIAM LLOYD GARRISON: Abolitionist Journalist

The gods smiled on Lloyd Garrison when a friend told him about a job opening at the local newspaper office. The time was October 1818; the place, Newburyport, Massachusetts.

Life had been hard for this 12-year-old. His seaman father had sailed away and never returned. His fragile, near-destitute mother had put him in the care of relatives and neighbors more than once. His schooling was cut short when he had to earn money for his caretakers' coffers.

Eight years later Garrison emerged from an apprenticeship with Ephraim W. Allen, owner of the *Newburyport Herald,* as a skillful, witty, politically astute young man. In the interim he had become an expert typesetter, compositor, and pressman and had even tried his hand at writing. Thanks to the Allen family's library, he had read his way to an education (typical of the time, he lived with the master's family). And he had adopted the view that the independent press was, in Allen's words, "a safeguard for freedom."

Garrison Goes Rogue By 1829 the journalist now known as William Lloyd Garrison was advocating for temperance and pacifism in print. Then Benjamin Lundy, publisher of *The Genius of Universal Emancipation* in Baltimore, won him over to abolitionism. Garrison took over the paper for six months and transformed both the *Genius* and himself. In the process he brought to the antislavery movement a radicalism rarely seen.

Garrison's prim look belied his radicalism.

The Liberator After moving to Boston, Garrison began lecturing against colonization, a plan he rejected after taking the writings of northern black abolitionists to heart. Then, with the aid of supporters, he founded the newspaper that would trumpet the abolitionist cause for 35 years, a record never bested: *The Liberator*—the first issue of which arrived on January 1, 1831. In his manifesto on page 1, Garrison famously positioned himself as an uncompromising voice against slavery: "I am in earnest—I will not equivocate—I will not excuse—I will not retreat a single inch—AND I WILL BE HEARD."

☛ FREDERICK DOUGLASS: The Voice of His People

Frederick Augustus Washington Bailey was born a slave in Talbot County, Maryland, around 1818. At age eight he was sent by his master to Baltimore to work for Hugh Auld, who managed a shipbuilding concern at Fells Point. Fred's task was to look after Auld's son Tommy.

Auld's kindly wife Sophia began to teach Fred to read and spell. Then, as literacy's light began to dawn, Hugh Auld halted the lessons. "If you teach that n----r how to read," the man who would become Frederick Douglass later wrote of Auld's order, "there would be no keeping him. It would forever unfit him to be a slave."

Auld's words rang only too true, and Fred was steeled with purpose. He befriended white boys in the neighborhood who, though poor and underfed, had the luxury of schooling. Finishing his errands in short order left time for impromptu reading lessons, and Fred gave the boys bread from the Auld pantry in return.

Fred's Flight to Freedom In 1833 Fred was taken from the Auld household and returned to the Talbot County plantation, where he worked the fields. After enduring three years of whippings and worse, he was sent back to Baltimore, bringing with him a desperate desire for freedom.

Douglass went from fugitive to freedman in 1846.

The Aulds hired Fred out to a caulker at the Fells Point wharves, and as he mastered the job, he also made good use of spare time. He attended meetings of a debating club for free black men. He courted and fell in love with a free black housekeeper named Anna Murray. And all the while, he was "ever on the lookout for a means of escape."

The moment of truth arrived on September 3, 1838. Disguised as a sailor and carrying papers lent by a free black, Fred traveled northward from Baltimore by train and boat to Philadelphia, then on to New York City.

New York to New Bedford His first stop was the home of David Ruggles, who welcomed him with open arms and, with other Underground Railroad operatives (page 50), arranged for him and soon-to-arrive Anna to travel to the maritime city of New Bedford, Massachusetts—a likely place to put his caulking skills to work. After their marriage under Ruggles's roof, the newlyweds were delivered to the home of New Bedford abolitionist Nathan Johnson, who helped usher Fred into a life unchained.

Bailey to Johnson to Douglass

David Ruggles had advised newly escaped slave Frederick Bailey to change his surname for the sake of safety. Fred chose Johnson. In a matter of days, Nathan Johnson of New Bedford agreed the name Bailey had to go, but doubted the wisdom of a man so impressive becoming "just another Johnson" in a city full of Johnsons.

"I gave Mr. Johnson the privilege of choosing me a name...." Fred later wrote. "He had just been reading the 'Lady of the Lake,' and at once suggested that my name be Douglass"—who, as a member of an "exiled race" in Sir Walter Scott's poem, was "hunted like a stag." Eight years would pass until Frederick Douglass no longer risked capture, after British abolitionists purchased his freedom from master Hugh Auld of Baltimore.

A Career-Launching Speech It was a subscription to William Lloyd Garrison's *The Liberator* and, in turn, attendance at the August 1841 Massachusetts Anti-Slavery Society (MAS) convention in Nantucket that set Frederick Douglass on the road to fame.

Garrison took an active role at the gathering. At the close of one session, the tall, lean Douglass stood and asked to be recognized. Hesitancy gave way to eloquence as he spoke of his bondage and escape. The poetry in his words stunned the audience silent—and Garrison knew he had found a man who could advance the antislavery cause in giant steps.

Within weeks Douglass joined the MAS and began a lecture tour. His powers were such that some whispered he couldn't possibly be a slave. In his defense he published *The Narrative of the Life of Frederick Douglass, an American Slave, Written By Himself* (1845)—a title leaving no doubt that his words were his own.

☛ THE QUESTION OF BLACK COLONIZATION

The American Colonization Society (ACS), the brainchild of the Rev. Robert Finley of New Jersey, was formed in 1816 by northern Quakers and southern slaveholders. And therein lay the rub. Though most of the Northerners—including Reverend Finley's fellow clergymen and distinguished statesmen from the North and South alike—had the welfare of blacks in mind, the hidden aim of many slaveholders was not so charitable. Regardless, in 1821 the ACS purchased land on Africa's west coast and founded Liberia, where thousands of free blacks would settle.

Clashing Opinions The great majority of free blacks saw colonization as a slap in the face. Compare the views of leading figures from two different worlds:

- ★ Henry Clay, Speaker of the U.S. House of Representatives and a kindhearted slaveholder, believed that given the "unconquerable prejudice resulting from [free blacks'] color, they could never amalgamate with the free whites in this country."

- ★ Wealthy (and black) Philadelphia businessman James Forten resented the notion that people who had helped build the "land of the free" should uproot themselves. "To separate the blacks from the whites," he said, "is as impossible as to bale out the Delaware [River] with a bucket."

☛ JAMES FORTEN: A "Success" Story

He was born free in Philadelphia 10 years before the Declaration of Independence was signed. And in Philadelphia, James Forten would stay. Apprenticed to a white sailmaker, he learned his trade well. When his master sold him the business, Forten built on his ready-made customer base and a reputation for superior craftsmanship. His real estate and railroad investments brought him riches, but even the wealthiest black man could go only so far in nineteenth-century America.

Naked Prejudice Though Forten gained the respect of his white clients and employees, discrimination was evident at every turn.

★ When he told a recently elected congressman he had marched his white journeymen to the polls to vote in his favor, the inability of Forten himself to cast a vote hung in the air.

★ The cartoons of artist Edward W. Clay portrayed Philadelphia's black elite as buffoons with exaggerated features, pretentious and ill-matched clothing, and speech peppered with word mix-ups.

Achievement within Limits It was in Philadelphia's black community that Forten flourished as a leader and abolitionist. (The Pennsylvania Abolition Society—the nation's oldest—admitted whites only.) He often was the first to chair meetings and draft petitions, including one demanding an end to the slave trade. Forten also published *Letters from a Man of Color* (1813), an attack on legislation proposing to limit the rights of black Pennsylvanians. He later contributed significant financial aid to William Lloyd Garrison as the radical journalist prepared to publish *The Liberator*.

The Forten Women Forten's wife, Charlotte, and their three daughters were activists in their own right. In 1833 they helped famed Quaker social reformer Lucretia Mott found the Philadelphia Female Anti-Slavery Society, the country's first bi-racial women's abolitionist group. Margaretta, a teacher, opened her own school in 1850 and worked for women's rights. Sarah wrote poems and articles for *The Liberator*. Harriet married abo-litionist Robert Purvis and worked long and hard for the cause. Her distinguished husband helped William Lloyd Garrison found the American Anti-Slavery Society (page 58) and would become its longest-serving member.

☛ JAMES G. BIRNEY: Southerner Founds Antislavery Party!

James G. Birney: esteemed lawyer and abolitionist

In the 1830s Kentucky-born James Gillespie Birney vied with William Lloyd Garrison for prominence in the abolitionist realm. A forthright man of wealth and great reputation, Birney left the law profession, freed the slaves on his Alabama cotton plantation, and began publishing *The Philanthropist*, an antislavery paper, in Cincinnati.

In 1838 Birney was elected to the executive commit-tee of American Anti-Slavery Society (AASS), founded by Garrison. Though the two shared a belief in immediate eman-cipation, Birney soon split with Garrison and his followers, or Garrisonians, over three main issues: the Garrisonians' pref-erence for "moral suasion" (page 58) over political action to lessen the adverse effects of the slave system, their support of disunion (separating the northern states from the South), and their demand to include woman's suffrage in the AASS platform.

J. P. Ball, Daguerreotypist

The daguerreotypist James Presley Ball, born free in Virginia and known as J.P., was 20 years old when he opened a studio in Cincinnati in 1845. As his photography business grew, some of the most famous abolitionists of the time were among his customers.

In 1855 came his greatest feat, in collaboration with black painters including the esteemed Robert Duncanson—a 2,400-square-yard canvas with a title to match: *Mammoth Pictorial Tour of the United States Comprising Views of the African Slave Trade; of Northern and Southern Cities; of Cotton and Sugar Plantations; of the Mississippi, Ohio and Susquehanna Rivers, Niagara Falls & etc.* The panorama was exhibited in Cincinnati and Boston. Accompanying it was a pamphlet describing "the horrors of slavery from capture in Africa through middle pass to bondage," written by Cincinnati printer and abolitionist Achilles Pugh.

Ball would also document black life from the antebellum years through the war and Reconstruction. It is said that his photography kept untold numbers of families connected to their soldier fathers and sons.

★ ★ ★ ★ ★ ★ ★ ★ ★ ★ ★ ★ CHRONICLERS ★ ★ ★ ★ ★ ★ ★ ★ ★ ★ ★ ★

The Liberty Party On Birney's bitter parting with the AASS in 1840, he and Gerrit Smith (page 57) founded the Liberty Party, whose platform was abolitionism. Birney failed badly in his 1844 run for president on the Liberty ticket. The party was soon absorbed into the Free Soil Party (page 61).

☛ JAMES McCUNE SMITH: Groundbreaking Physician

Bright, young James Smith, whose slave parents had fled from Virginia to New York, was given a spot at the city's African Free School—the progressive experiment of Alexander Hamilton, John Jay, and other dignitaries. After graduating, he moved to Scotland and earned BA, MA, and MD degrees from the University of Glasgow. Back home in New York, James McCune Smith became the first university-trained black physician in the United States.

At home in New York, Smith operated a successful medical practice for 25 years and opened two pharmacies in Lower Manhattan. He helped found the New York Society for Promotion of Education of Colored Children. And he served for more than 20 years as medical director of the Colored Orphan Asylum at Fifth Avenue and 42nd Street; the orphanage was burned to the ground in the Draft Riots of 1863 but was soon rebuilt in Harlem.

Though Smith did his share of public speaking, he preferred the written word, both as doctor and antislavery advocate. Smith's writings are collected in *The Works of James McCune Smith: Black Intellectual and Abolitionist* (2007).

Students of Rebellion

Some abolitionists calling for immediate emancipation took radicalism to higher level. Out-of-the-ordinary schooling set the stage for all three of these impassioned activists, each of whom made his mark.

☛ HENRY HIGHLAND GARNET: Provocateur and Preacher

In the late 1820s Henry Garnet's family escaped from Maryland to New York City, where Henry entered the African Free School (page 29). In 1835 he left for Canaan, New Hampshire, to pursue higher education at the new Noyes Academy, an interracial school founded by Canaan's abolition sympathizers. Five months later townspeople, alarmed by "racemixing," voted to shut the academy down, and within days a mob attacked and destroyed it.

"Liberty or Death!" The already radical Garnet was now even more fervid. He became a minister who brandished the slogan "Liberty or Death!" At the 1843 Black National Convention in Buffalo, New York, he gave his "Address to the Slaves of the

United States," also known as the Call to Rebellion speech. And after the war, he ruled a fiery pulpit at New York City's Shiloh Presbyterian Church in Harlem.

Late in life, Highland chose to act on his support for colonization, and he moved to Liberia (page 26). He sailed and settled, but died only two months later. He lies buried at Palm Grove Cemetery, in the capital city of Monrovia.

☛ MARTIN DELANY: Black Nationalist

Born free and of pure African stock in 1812, the radical abolitionist Martin Delany did anything and everything, from founding a society for the education of young black men to coediting Frederick Douglass's *North Star* to studying at Harvard Medical School until his fellow students objected to his presence. (He later settled into dentistry.) Delany is better known for his black nationalism. His book *The Condition, Elevation, Emigration, and Destiny of the Colored People of the United States, Politically Considered* (1852) urged American blacks to build a new nation in Africa or the Caribbean. His exploratory travels to Nigeria resulted in a treaty to establish settlements in a wilderness area, but it collapsed when warfare broke out in both Nigeria and the United States.

☛ THOMAS WENTWORTH HIGGINSON: Phi Beta Kappa

Born into a long line of prominent Massachusetts families, Thomas Wentworth Higginson entered Harvard at age 13. He was lonely, awkward at six feet tall, and full of anxiety that he wouldn't excel. Yet he made Phi Beta Kappa. He went on to the Harvard Divinity School, dropped out to pursue a literary career, and returned once he realized that "poetic genius is utterly foreign to me." In 1847 he took the pulpit at a Unitarian church in Newburyport. His advocacy for better wages for local workers and freedom for the slaves made his conservative parishioners uncomfortable enough to dismiss him two years later.

The Boston Court House was a magnet for antislavery protestors.

Incident at the Boston Court House In 1854 Higginson employed the radical action he embraced as the way to end the godlessness of slavery. Using a 14-foot pole as a battering ram, he led an assault on the Boston Court House, where fugitive slave Anthony Burns (page 54) was jailed. The raid failed, but a deputy sherrif was killed when someone fired a gun. Higginson, who proclaimed a revolution had begun, was indicted for treason. The charges were later dropped.

Bomb Throwers

Other emancipationists actually called the slaves to rebellion. One was a free black merchant in Boston; the other was a radical enraged by the fallout of the Kansas-Nebraska Act.

☛ DAVID WALKER: Provocative Pamphleteer

In September 1829 freeborn David Walker, a North Carolinian who had become a store owner and activist in Boston, wrote himself into the history books with a pamphlet alternately described as "present[ing] the first sustained critique of slavery and racism in the United States by an African person" and "for a brief and terrifying moment...the most notorious document in America." The document was *David Walker's Appeal, in Four Articles: Together with a Preamble to the Coloured Citizens of the World, but in Particular, and Very Expressly, to Those of the United States of America.* Hatred of slavery ran deep in Walker's veins. As a child, he beheld, among other horrors, a young slave forced to literally whip the life out of his mother. The purpose of the *Appeal* was to rouse slaves to rebellion. "They want us to be their slaves," Walker wrote, "and think nothing of murdering us...and believe this, that it is no more harm for you to kill a man who is trying to kill you than it is for you to take a drink of water when thirsty."

Response to the *Appeal* Reaction in the South to Walker's *Appeal* was swift. Slaves saw in it a ray of hope. Whites put a $3,000 bounty on Walker's head, and the legislatures of states in the North, South, and West either passed or dusted off legislation barring the teaching of slaves to read and write. The same went for laws banning the distribution of antislavery literature.

A passionate Christian, Walker called abolition a "glorious and heavenly cause." He sought immediate emancipation, condemned colonization, and saw the avowal in the Declaration of Independence that "all men are created equal" as applicable to every American.

Suspicious Death? His *Appeal* energized early black and white abolitionists, but Walker would not see the dream fulfilled. He was found dead at his home in August 1830—possibly from poisoning, as many believed at the time. Some historians suspect he was more likely felled by the same disease that killed his daughter: tuberculosis.

☛ THE FATEFUL KANSAS-NEBRASKA ACT

Slave and free states had maintained a precarious balance after the Compromise of 1850 (page 18), but the Kansas-Nebraska Act repealed the Missouri Compromise of 1820, which allowed slavery in the territory north of the 36° 30´ latitude. Introduced by Sen. Stephen Douglas of Illinois, the new act stated that the issue of slavery would be decided by popular sovereignty—a vote by the people. After the bill passed on May 30, 1854, violence erupted as Free Staters from the North and proslavery guerrillas joined the fight to determine whether the territory would join the Union as a free or slave state.

Slave Power At the root of the conflict was so-called slave power. For years, northern Federalists had protested the South's weight in national politics, thanks to additional representation granted to slaveholders by the three-fifths clause of the Constitution. (When population numbers were calculated to determine congressional representation and direct taxation, a slave was counted as three-fifths of a free person.) The population of the free states outnumbered that of slave states two to one, yet they enjoyed only a 25 percent advantage in the Electoral College.

☛ JOHN BROWN: Madman or Hero?

In 1849 John Brown called on Gerrit Smith, bought 244 acres at "Timbucto" (page 57) at a dollar an acre, and moved his family from Massachusetts to North Elba, New York. Taking part in this experiment was a new start for Brown, who had endured a long string of failed businesses and bankruptcies. He was a man of strong passions, having been raised in a strictly religious, fervently abolitionist home in Torrington, Connecticut, where he was born in 1800. So it came as no surprise that Brown and four of his sons joined into the battle that erupted in Kansas in the wake of the Kansas-Nebraska Act of 1854.

An Eye on Harpers Ferry John Brown had long fantasized about a wandering guerilla force that would somehow free the slaves. And in January 1857 he traveled to Boston to seek support from antislavery sympathizers—the group who would become known as the Secret Six.

Brown outlined only the bare bones: An attack on the federal arsenal at Harpers Ferry, Virginia, by blacks and whites would incite slaves from across the South to escape and then join him in safe havens in the Allegheny Mountains. There he would arm and train them for guerilla warfare. The loss of slaves and fear of further insurrection, he said, would destabilize the South and build support for abolition in the North.

Brown's Doomed Raid On October 16, 1859, Brown led 21 men—16 whites (including three of his sons) and five blacks—to the arsenal, all assigned to different tasks. They successfully captured three buildings, but plans soon went awry. A local mob surrounded the town, leaving Brown and his raiders holed up. Then, two days later, Robert E. Lee and other Union soldiers stormed the arsenal. In the earlier skirmishes, a total of 10 men had been killed, including two of Brown's sons.

An idealized painting of John Brown leaving for his execution shows him as a martyr caught between slavery and the law.

Brown was tried for conspiracy to incite a slave insurrection, treason against Virginia, and murder. At his trial, he declared his act was God's will: "To have interfered as I have done...in behalf of His despised poor, I did not wrong, but right." John Brown was hanged on December 2, 1859.

WIELDERS OF THE WORD

Advances in printing technology made it easier for antislavery
writers to make their case in books and abolitionist newspapers.
Their public-speaker counterparts traveled the country to
address audiences in lecture halls, and the voices of
antislavery ministers rang out in church.

———— ((O)) ————

On the Page

The debate over slavery intensified on the printed page. One author took on the issue as never before, an antislavery journalist
died for the cause, and a Mrs. Stowe penned a history-making
novel. On a very different page, a politician put forth biblical
justifications for slavery.

☛ LYDIA MARIA CHILD: Doyenne of Domesticity to Radical

It was hardly her Thanksgiving poem "Over the River and
Through the Woods" that made Lydia Maria Child a household
name in her day. It was her inventive mind and productivity.
Her novel *Hobomok, A Tale of Early Times* (1824) was the first
sympathetic treatment of America's native peoples. The magazine she launched in 1826—*The Juvenile Miscellany*—set the
standard for children's periodicals. *The Frugal Housewife* (1829)
and *The Mother's Book* (1931) bettered the lives of countless
low-income housewives and mothers.

In 1828 Maria Francis married David Child, editor of
Boston's *Massachusetts Journal*, a publication of the Conscience
Whigs (the Whig Party's antislavery faction). As fate would have
it, William Lloyd Garrison worked briefly at the *Journal,* and the
more Mrs. Child read of Garrison's radical abolitionist views,
the more she investigated the "Negro question."

Mrs. Child's Fall from Grace The year 1833 saw publication of her fearlessly frank *Appeal in Favor of That Class of Americans Called Africans,* said by some modern-day scholars to be the volume from which all other abolitionist books derived. Woven through the *Appeal* was a reasoned criticism of racial prejudice.

The *Appeal* incensed Child's adoring readers. Demand for her books and children's magazine died on the vine, and many of her closest friends deserted her. At the same time, the *Appeal* had a lasting effect on a number of brilliant young thinkers—among them Wendell Phillips (page 43), Thomas Wentworth Higginson, and the poet John Greenleaf Whittier.

Antebellum slavery literature excluded John Greenleaf Whittier's poem "Our Countrymen in Chains" (1837) with its fitting cover illustration.

Onward and Upward

If Child lost her public, she discovered her calling for reform.

★ Her *History of the Condition of Women* (1835) helped spur the suffrage movement and was praised by Elizabeth Cady Stanton as an essential resource in the fight for women's rights.

★ From 1840 onward her writings in *The National Anti-Slavery Standard* and other publications shed new light on the need for social reform.

Child vs. the Governor Among the acquaintances of Lydia Maria Child was John Brown. As the rabid abolitionist lay in a Virginia prison cell awaiting execution after the raid at Harpers Ferry, Child wrote Gov. Henry A. Wise and asked permission to visit her friend. The governor granted her request in a letter dripping with sarcasm and condescension. He also suggested, in so many words, that Child and her kind shared Brown's guilt.

Child's letter to Governor Wise somehow found its way into the pages of the New York *Tribune*. Meanwhile, her blistering reply to the governor, complete with glorification of the abolition-ist cause and indictments of slavery, hypocrisy, and imperialism, elicited an angry letter from the wife of James Mason, the sena-tor from Virginia. Child's response to Mrs. Mason soared to even greater rhetorical heights.

> **The governor granted her request in a letter dripping with sarcasm....**

William Lloyd Garrison found these debates by pen so note-worthy he published them in a pamphlet and printed 300,000 copies. Today the letters live on in book form, under the title *Correspondence Between Lydia Maria Child and Gov. Wise and Mrs. Mason, of Virginia.*

☛ ELIJAH P. LOVEJOY: Martyr to the Cause

Born into a religiously moral family in Maine, Elijah Parish Lovejoy graduated at the head of this class at Waterville Col-lege (now Colby), became a minister, and then grew obsessed with abolition. And he was buried on his thirty-fifth birthday, murdered by a mob.

Lovejoy spread the word through *The Observer,* his abo-litionist paper. And wherever he lived, mobs destroyed his printing press. From Albion, Maine, he moved to St. Louis and then across the river to Alton, Illinois. It was here, after Lovejoy took delivery of a new press, that a mob attacked on the night of

November 7, 1837. As a mixed group of town leaders and ruffians wrecked the press and tossed its parts into the river, Lovejoy was shot dead.

His murder and its aftermath buoyed people of great power and strengthened abolitionists. In the end, the travesty made it difficult for the public to separate the liberty to write about slavery from the liberty of the enslaved. Abolitionism also gained a somewhat firmer foothold in the mainstream press. "The press, we are rejoiced to say," read an editorial in Pennsylvania's *Easton Whig*, "utters one common sentiment of abhorrence at this bloody transaction."

Assault on the Abolitionist Press

While some mobs descending on abolitionist newspapermen were surely little more than proslavery rowdies, the instigators were usually a town's most upstanding citizens. And this was the case in Alton, Illinois. It was not Elijah Lovejoy's attackers who were arrested and tried but rather his defenders and the owner of the building where the press was housed.

Common law doctrines of the antebellum period were community oriented, giving local authorities the freedom to regulate speech violating community standards. Majority rights took precedence over individual rights, and majorities often thought it necessary to quiet antislavery voices they deemed not only radical but dangerous.

Those dangers to society included journalist William Lloyd Garrison, who in 1835 narrowly escaped lynching for speaking out against the immorality of slavery from both the platform and *The Liberator;* Cincinnati publisher James G. Birney, whose *Philanthropist* print shop and press were attacked twice in July 1836 and destroyed in September 1841; and Kentuckian Cassius M. Clay, who protected his *True American* office with a cannon and, in 1846, watched as his press was dismantled and shipped to the free state of Ohio by court order.

☛ HARRIET BEECHER STOWE:
"The Little Woman Who Started This Great War"

The girl called Hattie was petite, pretty, and quite smart. She was bookish, too, with a special love of the poems of Lord Byron. At age 21 she would move from Litchfield, Connecticut, to Cincinnati when her father, the famous revivalist preacher Lyman Beecher, assumed the presidency of Lane Theological Seminary.

Cincinnati was only a riverbank away from the slave state of Kentucky. The Beechers harbored runaway slaves on occasion; Harriet opened a Sunday school for black children; and she befriended Eliza Buck, who helped her with housework and told shocking stories of her former life as a slave.

Harriet Beecher married Calvin Stowe, the seminary's only professor, in 1836. He encouraged her dabblings with the pen, including sketches of New England life for *Godey's Lady's Book*. It was a sister-in-law who praised her writing and suggested she write "something that will make this whole nation feel what an accursed thing slavery is."

Stowe wrote Gamaliel Bailey, editor of *The New Era*, an antislavery magazine in Washington, D.C., and proposed a serialized tale of slavery. What was intended as a few installments of *Uncle Tom's Cabin, or Life Among the Lowly* numbered 40 in the end. Published in two volumes in 1852, the book would go on be translated into 60 languages and achieve sales second only to the Bible.

Pictures of the characters from Uncle Tom's Cabin *flooded the market in the 1850s.*

Praise and Rancor for Stowe Stowe's emotional rendering of the slave's humanity—the Christlike Uncle Tom, the courageous fugitive Eliza—reached the general public as no antislavery publication had before. She also brought to life slaveholders at two extremes: the kindhearted Arthur Shelby and the demonic Simon Legree. Not surprisingly, reviews in the North and South took a very different tone, as in these two excerpts:

> "With a careful unexaggerating fidelity to facts that the Southerner must accept, [the book] unites an outspoken energy and fearlessness of portraiture that the Northerner must feel."
>
> — *The Independent*

> "We beg to make a single suggestion to Mrs. Stowe— that, as she is fond of referring the Bible, she will turn over, before writing her next book of fiction, to the twentieth chapter of Exodus and there read these words—THOU SHALT NOT BEAR FALSE WITNESS AGAINST THY NEIGHBOR."
>
> — *The Southern Literary Messenger*

The hue and cry from proslavery Americans was so loud that Stowe wrote an entire book to refute them: *A Key to Uncle Tom's Cabin, Presenting the Original Facts and Documents Upon Which the Story Is Founded* (1853).

It is said that on welcoming Mrs. Stowe to the White House, President Lincoln greeted her with "So this is the little woman who made this great war." The story may be unsubstantiated, but there is no disputing that Harriet Beecher Stowe's 312-page novel helped lay the groundwork for the war.

Stowe's Uncle Tom? In *A Key to Uncle Tom's Cabin*, Harriet Beecher Stowe noted a few "parallels" to her fictional (and suddenly famous) Uncle Tom, and Josiah Henson was one of them. In 1849 Henson's *The Life of Josiah Henson, Former Slave* had recounted his story of escape and profound religiosity so vividly that 300,000 copies were sold. Four years later Henson proceeded to go on a lecture tour as the living inspiration for Stowe's Uncle Tom, and the third edition of his narrative was titled *Uncle Tom's Story of His Life* (1875).

Whether the character of the best-selling book of its time was based on Henson is open to question. Stowe wrote the preface to Henson's second edition of his biography, *Truth Stranger Than Fiction: Father Henson's Story of His Own Life* (1858), though without any suggestion that Tom grew from Henson. Furthermore, in a letter archived at the Harriet Beecher Stowe Center in Hartford, Connecticut, Stowe states that Henson was not the model for Tom.

☛ T. HOWELL COBB: Slavery and the Bible

The use of the Bible to justify slavery knew no geographical bounds. Sweden-born Rabbi Morris Jacob Raphall's treatise "The Bible View of Slavery" (1861) was read and argued around the world. In antebellum America, Georgia native Howell T. Cobb,

Thomas Howell Cobb addresses the Confederate senate in Montgomery, Alabama. The capital moved to Richmond in late May, 1861.

who served as Speaker of the U.S. House of Representatives and the fortieth governor of his state, weighed in with *A Scriptural Examination of the Institution of Slavery* (1856). In the preface, Cobb held that "Slavery, as it exists in the United States, is the Providentially-arranged means whereby Africa is to be lifted from her deep degradation, to a state of civil and religious liberty."

In 1860 Cobb switched his allegiance from the Union to the secession movement. As a general in the Confederate army, he saw action in the Peninsula Campaign and the Battle of Antietam. He also suggested that a prisoner-of-war camp be built in southern Georgia; a camp soon rose in the red earth outside Andersonville

---

From Platform and Pulpit

In the golden age of oratory, lecturers regularly toured the country to speak on the issues of the day. Three antislavery lecturers or clergymen who gained fame were a New England aristocrat, a black poet turned public speaker, and a silver-tongued Boston Unitarian minister.

☛ WENDELL PHILLIPS: Brahmin Radical

Few men were as favored as Wendell Phillips, born in 1811 to a family that had achieved high standing in the realms of the clergy, commerce, and education. Yet he devoted his life to the least favored—the enslaved.

It was this Boston Brahmin's nature to go against the grain, and after earning a Harvard law degree, he was drawn to abolitionism. In turn, he spoke at the occasional antislavery meeting. Then came his shining moment. Elijah Lovejoy (page 38) had been murdered in Illinois 27 days earlier, and a local pastor had called a meeting of condemnation at Faneuil Hall. At one point

Massachusetts attorney general James T. Austin denounced the "abstractions" that had been uttered in the hall and claimed Lovejoy's killers ("patriots," he called them) merely exercised a neighborly duty to uphold the laws and prejudices of a slave state.

Wendell Phillips, four-star orator

Phillips Talks Back

Phillips stood at once, and his wholly off-the-cuff counterstatement caused a sensation. In mid-speech he pointed to portraits of the founding fathers and said, "I thought those those pictured lips would have broken into voice to rebuke [Austin]…For the sentiments [he] uttered on soil consecrated by the prayers and blood of patriots, the earth should have yawned and swallowed him up."

Within days Phillips traded the practice of law for abolitionism. He became one of the most sought-after speakers on the lecture circuit and succeeded William Lloyd Garrison as president of the American Anti-Slavery Society.

☛ FRANCES WATKINS HARPER: Poet to Lecturer

Born free in Baltimore in 1825, Frances Ellen Watkins was given an education most Caucasian schoolgirls would have envied. She delved into Greek, Latin, philosophy, and biblical studies at the Academy for Negro Youth, founded by her uncle—the Rev. William Watkins, a noted abolitionist. With his wife Henrietta, the good reverend raised Frances from age two following the death of her mother.

The art of writing came easy to Frances, who was smitten by poetry. Her second book—*Poems on Miscellaneous Subjects* (1854)—went through 20 printings.

A Poet Transformed With the advent of the Fugitive Slave Act of 1850, abolitionists grew more fervent and the Underground Railroad gained steam. At the same time, fear among whites escalated in the North and South. Maryland tightened enforcement of an 1840 law subjecting nonresident free blacks to enslavement. In November an "alien" free black broke the law and was arrested, shackled, and transported to Georgia. After escaping, he was caught, only to die from what was recorded in Maryland as "exposure and suffering." Frances Watkins, who had moved to Ohio and then Pennsylvania to teach school, was horrified to think she might meet a similar fate for the simple act of going home to visit friends and family in her home state. "Upon that grave," she later wrote, "I pledged myself to the antislavery cause."

The Activist Gets Busy Moving to Philadelphia, home to the nation's highest concentration of freemen, Watkins observed activity at an Underground Railroad station and attended antislavery meetings. Her next stop was New Bedford, Massachusetts, a hive of abolitionist activity. Here she began a public-speaking career with the lecture "The Education and Elevation of the Colored Race." The Maine Anti-Slavery Society soon hired Watkins to lecture in the northern states and Canada.

Watkins's marriage to widower Fenton Harper, in 1860, ended with his death four years later. Though she was left with three stepchildren and a daughter of her own, Mrs. F. E. W. Harper continued to write, lecture, and push for wartime and postwar reforms. Her stature was such that F. E. W. Harper Leagues—service clubs founded by black women—stayed active long after Harper's death in 1911.

☞ THEODORE PARKER: Immortal Wordsmith

If Theodore Parker fearlessly wielded the power of words, he came by it honestly. His grandfather, Capt. John Parker, wielded

Theodore Parker went from congregationalist minister to Unitarian minister to secular freethinker.

the first sword in the American Revolution as commander of the Minutemen on Lexington Green. The blunt Harvard-educated Reverend Parker talked himself out of a congregational pulpit after he repeatedly sermonized about the evils of slavery.

As pastor of his own Unitarian church in the Boston suburb of Roxbury, Parker had the sympathetic ear of such antislavery luminaries as William Lloyd Garrison, Elizabeth Cady Stanton, and Julia Ward Howe. He had met Howe and her husband, Samuel Gridley Howe, in Rome in 1844—12 years before he and Sam Howe would help fund John Brown's raid at Harper's Ferry as part of the so-called Secret Six.

A Passage to Remember Reverend Parker left behind passages that still resound. In fact, he wrote the words paraphrased by Martin Luther King, Jr.: "I do not pretend to understand the moral universe. The arc is a long one. My eye reaches but little ways, [but] I can divine [the curve] by conscience. And from what I see I am sure it bends toward justice."

Up from Slavery

Fugitive slaves joined whites and free blacks in efforts to end slavery as the nation expanded ever westward. Some, like Harriet Tubman, also symbolized the fight.

——— ◈ ———

Beyond the Stereotypes

The slave system was hardly confined to the South. Nor was abolitionism unknown there—especially before 1820 and the rise of King Cotton and the growing demand for slaves.

☞ SLAVERY IN THE NORTH

Slavery was a fact of life in early America, and it didn't fade away in the North until well into the nineteenth century. Northern states passed emancipation laws under the terms of gradualism, a decades-long process. For instance, in 1799 the New York legislature passed "An Act for the Gradual Abolition of Slavery." Modeled on Pennsylvania's law of 1780, it specified the following:

★ Slavery would end on July 4, 1827.

★ Slaves born before 1799 would be freed unconditionally on that date.

★ Those born after 1799 were obligated, barring manumission (deeded emancipation by their masters), to remain indentured until they were 28-years-old if male, 25-years-old if female.

Terms varied by state; the emancipation ages in Rhode Island, for instance, were 21 years old for males, 18 years old for females.

☞ ABOLITIONISM IN THE SOUTH

There is no doubt that untold numbers of whites harbored antislavery sentiments in the antebellum South. The question is whether significant abolitionist movements existed and if the individual activists who made it into the history books, including Cassius M. Clay (page 58), did so because they were far and few between.

> [Southern abolitionist societies] shared the same risks: the ever-present threat of being ostracized, mobbed, or shut down.

Valiant Efforts For all that, Southern antislavery advocates *tried*—and the more their efforts became known in the North, the more the case for emancipation was bolstered. In 1807 the Kentucky Abolitionist Society was formed as an offshoot of the Baptized Licking-Locust Association, Friends of Humanity confederation—emancipationist Baptist churches brought together by Rev. David Barrow. (One member was Thomas Lincoln, father of the future president.) In 1820 Elihu Embree of Jonesville, Tennessee, published *The Emancipator,* one of the first abolitionist newspapers in the nation.

Thomas Lincoln, father of President Abraham Lincoln

Other abolitionist publications and societies popped up in the border states, usually at the instigation of Quakers or Methodists. If they were pale ghosts of their northern counterparts—and adhered to the doctrine of gradual, rather than immediate, emancipation—they shared the same risks: the ever-present threat of being ostracized, mobbed, or shut down.

The Underground Railroad

In the early 1830s the people who helped runaway slaves make their way north came to be known collectively as the Underground Railroad. Here you'll meet some of the most notable "conductors" and "stationmasters."

☛ JUST WHAT WAS IT?

The Underground Railroad had no official organizers, much less a headquarters. Instead it consisted of a loose network of antislavery sympathizers who harbored fugitive slaves fleeing to the northern states or Canada. These men and women—some white, some black—usually knew little of the larger operation but did their part to ease the move of hundreds of slaves northward each year.

The Quakers Levi and Catharine Coffin took more than 3,000 slaves into their stations (safe houses) in Newport, Indiana, and Cincinnati between 1826 and 1863. The Rev. Calvin Fairbank was imprisoned twice for conducting slaves to freedom in Kentucky. Others who aided the flight of slaves were never identified or chose to remain anonymous. Who knows whether any of the Quakers who helped a young slave negotiate a hundred-mile journey from Maryland to freedom—namely, Harriet Tubman (page 50), who is forever linked to the Underground Railroad—knew they were part of a group or merely acted because they saw a person in need?

☛ DAVID RUGGLES: New York Accomplice

In New York City, David Ruggles's three-story town house—at 36 Lispenard Street in present-day Tribeca—was a key Underground Railroad stop on the route to upstate New York and New England. It also housed what is said to be America's first black bookstore and black-owned printing press. Here Ruggles put out untold numbers of antislavery pamphlets and welcomed not only fugitive slaves but also leading abolitionists of both races.

Born in Connecticut in 1810, Ruggles moved to New York around 1825 and worked as a seaman and a grocer. In a time when blacks were frequently kidnapped off street corners and sold into slavery, he began to direct his energies to abolitionism full-time. He was a founding member of the New York Committee of Vigilance and, by his estimate, aided as many as 600 fugitive slaves. Frederick Douglass wrote of "the humane hand of Mr. David Ruggles, whose vigilance, kindness, and perseverance I shall never forget."

☛ WILLIAM STILL: Philadelphia Pioneer

Born free on a farm in Burlington County, New Jersey, in 1821, William Still moved to Philadelphia in his early twenties. He would find success as a coal stove merchant, but his more important work was as head of the vigilance committee aiding fugitive slaves. Still ignored the risks as he sheltered up to 60 slaves a month. He also left a great gift for Civil War scholars when he meticulously recorded his charges' stories. His book *The Underground Railroad* (1872) relayed the experiences of more than 600 slaves—including Harriet Tubman. Still is remembered as one of the most dynamic leaders the Underground Railroad and is called by many its "father."

☛ HARRIET TUBMAN: The Fugitive Who Became an Icon

Born in Maryland in 1822, Araminta Ross—who later took her mother's name, Harriet—showed signs of selflessness from childhood. When she refused to help an overseer tie up an unruly black boy, she suffered the head injury that would plague her for a lifetime—a blow with a two-pound iron. Thereafter, her bouts of narcolepsy led masters and playmates alike to think

Harriet stupid. "But that brain which seems so dull," wrote her first biographer Sarah Bradford, "was full of busy thoughts."

Harriet Tubman's Escape Harriet married a freedman named John Tubman in 1844. When word came that she and her brothers might be sold and sent to the Deep South, she chose freedom. After traveling close to a hundred miles by the power of unflinching will and the kindness of strangers, she finally "crossed the line of which [she] had so long been dreaming." Bradford quotes her further:

> "I was free; but there was no one to welcome me to the land of freedom, I was a stranger in a strange land…But to this solemn resolution I came…I would make a home for my family in the North, and the Lord helping me, I would bring them all there."

An Unlikely Heroine Harriet Tubman settled in Philadelphia, fired with determination to rescue her family and other slaves. That she succeeded against all odds is at the root of her enduring legend. She was a woman. She was barely five feet tall. She was bedeviled by narcoleptic seizures. She was illiterate. Yet during her dozen or so missions she was never caught. And she never lost a slave.

Harriet Tubman—a tiny woman with a very large legacy

Tubman on the Rails

Tubman's early missions were independent. Once she became friends with two of the most active men of the Underground Railroad—Thomas Garret, a Wilmington Quaker known for channeling thousands of slaves into Pennsylvania, and William Still—she used the secretive network to her advantage.

In the mid-1850s she escorted slaves through upstate New York to Canada. Tubman herself spent her winters in St. Catharines, Ontario, where her much of her family had settled. In 1857 she fulfilled the vow she had made 13 years earlier and brought her elderly parents into the fold.

Three Who Made Waves

Two male slaves—Dred Scott and Anthony Burns—live on through their role in famous court cases. A female slave, Sojourner Truth, became known for the power of her voice.

☛ DRED SCOTT: Anonymous Litigant Gains Fame

History knows surprisingly little about a man whose name was attached to perhaps the most controversial Supreme Court decision of the nineteenth century. We know he was born Sam in Southampton County, Virginia, around 1795 but not why he changed his name to Dred; that he married a slave named Harriet Robinson in 1837; and that Scott was owned by Peter Blow, who moved his family to St. Louis in 1830.

After Blow's death in 1833, his daughter sold Scott to Dr. John Emerson, a military surgeon stationed south of St. Louis. Scott went with Emerson when the doctor was posted to Illinois territory, then Wisconsin—both free under the terms of the Missouri Compromise (page 18).

In 1842 Dr. Emerson, his wife Irene, and Scott returned to St. Louis. Emerson died the next year. Scott and his wife were now owned by Mrs. Emerson, and on June 30, 1847, *Dred Scott vs. Irene Emerson* went to court—the first step to the history-making decision of 1857.

The Scott Case's Mysterious Start From the beginning, partisans in the Dred Scott brouhaha argued over who made the decision to sue, and historians still debate the issue today. Was it Scott, who was illiterate and not given to rebellion, who took the lead? Was it his wife Harriet, as has recently been proposed? Was Scott used as a pawn in a test case orchestrated by abolitionists—in particular the late Peter Blow's son Henry (a lawyer) and perhaps even Irene Emerson herself—as one leading Civil War historian suggested? The number of attorneys who worked on the cases pro bono or charged minimal fees supports the ideological importance of the suits, and proslavery and antislavery Americans took sides regardless of who hatched the idea.

Scott vs. San[d]ford At issue in Scott vs. San[d]ford—the second, or Supreme Court, appeal—was whether a slave had the right to sue in federal court; whether extended residence in a free state meant the slave was freed; and whether the Missouri Compromise, which outlawed slavery in the Wisconsin Territory, was constitutional. In effect, a ruling in favor of the plaintiff would mean even free blacks with slave ancestry could never become a citizen. (The plaintiff's name is different from that in the original case because Irene Emerson transferred the title to Scott to her brother, John F. A. Sanford. In addition, a clerical error at some point added an extra *d* in Sanford's name for all time.)

A Stunning Decision After reviewing the case, the court handed down its decision on March 6, 1857. Seven of the justices ruled that because Scott was a slave rather than a citizen, he was powerless to sue in federal court; and the Missouri Compromise was unconstitutional, because Congress had no power to ban slavery in the territories.

Antislavery activists everywhere were stunned. In the end the court's decision raised the debate over slavery to the next level and moved the nation that much closer to war.

Roger B. Taney, Chief Justice

Roger B. Taney, the fifth Chief Justice of the Supreme Court, was born in 1777 on a tobacco plantation in Calvert County, Maryland. As a lawyer turned attorney general under Andrew Jackson, he had demonstrated his belief in state's rights but, in a paradox not unknown at the time, also freed his slaves.

Taney (pronounced TAW-nee) was 80 years old when he ruled against Dred Scott, and it was these few words that the world remembered: "Negroes had more than a century before [the Declaration of Independence] been regarded as beings of an inferior order, and altogether unfit to associate with the white race, either in social or political relations, and so far unfit that they had no rights which the white man was bound to respect."

Defenders at the time, and even today, hold that Taney merely stated what he believed to be the prevailing views of the late 1700s. But fairly or not, his reputation was forever stained.

★ ★ ★ ★ ★ ★ ★ ★ ★ ★ ★ ★   THE DISGRACED   ★ ★ ★ ★ ★ ★ ★ ★ ★ ★ ★ ★

☛ ANTHONY BURNS: Quasi-Defendant

As a slave owned by Charles Suttle of Alexandria, Burns, at times, almost felt free. Suttle allowed him to hire himself out, and Burns, in turn, supervised four other slaves hired out by Suttle. He learned to read and write, and he found religion and became a preacher. Still, he longed to escape from bondage.

While working in Richmond, Burns stowed away on a ship to Boston and found work with a tailor. When he wrote to his brother, the letter made its way to his master, who knew the law passed by Congress four years earlier would work in his favor.

On his arrival in Boston, master Charles Suttle had Burns arrested on a trumped-up charge of robbery. The true intent was to reclaim Burns under the terms of the Fugitive Slave Act. For a solid week, abolitionists both white and black held heated meetings, jammed the streets, and even attacked the courthouse in an attempt to rescue Burns. A small group of blacks led by

Thomas Wentworth Higginson (page 31) tried to batter down the courthouse door; they had made little more than a dent when a gun went off and a deputy sheriff guarding the building fell dead.

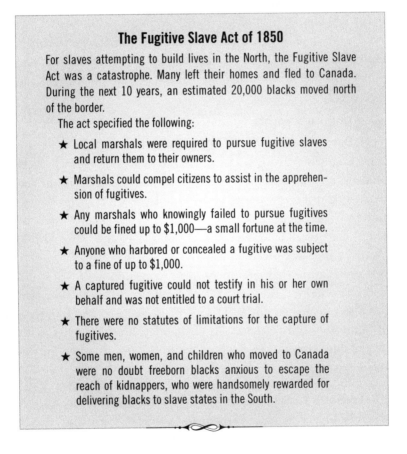

The Fugitive Slave Act of 1850

For slaves attempting to build lives in the North, the Fugitive Slave Act was a catastrophe. Many left their homes and fled to Canada. During the next 10 years, an estimated 20,000 blacks moved north of the border.

The act specified the following:

★ Local marshals were required to pursue fugitive slaves and return them to their owners.

★ Marshals could compel citizens to assist in the apprehension of fugitives.

★ Any marshals who knowingly failed to pursue fugitives could be fined up to $1,000—a small fortune at the time.

★ Anyone who harbored or concealed a fugitive was subject to a fine of up to $1,000.

★ A captured fugitive could not testify in his or her own behalf and was not entitled to a court trial.

★ There were no statutes of limitations for the capture of fugitives.

★ Some men, women, and children who moved to Canada were no doubt freeborn blacks anxious to escape the reach of kidnappers, who were handsomely rewarded for delivering blacks to slave states in the South.

The End of the Burns Saga The violence inside the courthouse where Burns was held was different from that outside. The Fugitive Slave Act left him stripped of all rights, and his forcible return to Virginia was a foregone conclusion. President

Franklin Pierce wanted to show that he was determined to execute the law, and ordered the troops to Boston to prove it.

On his way to the ship, Burns was marched down State Street in shackles, surrounded by enough soldiers to protect a miles-long convoy. The spectators outnumbered them, and doors and lampposts along the route were draped in black.

In time, good would come of the furor in Boston. A black church raised $1,300 to purchase Burns's freedom, and public opinion in the North turned against the brutal law.

☛ SOJOURNER TRUTH:
A Dutch-Speaking Slave Named Isabella

That Sojourner Truth spoke only Dutch for her first 17 years made it all the more remarkable that she became one of the most sought-after lecturers in the country. Born Isabella Baumfree in Ulster County, New York, which was peopled largely by Dutch farmers, she learned English only after she was sold to a family in nearby Kingston.

Isabella married another slave, Thomas, around 1815 and had five children. And in 1827 she not only received freedom but also a vision. As author Olive Gilbert wrote in *The Narrative of Sojourner Truth* (1850), "God revealed himself to her, with all the suddenness of a flash of lightning, showing her, 'in the twinkling of an eye, that he was all over.'"

Isabella to Sojourner Truth Another vision came in 1843 when Isabella changed her name to Sojourner Truth and set out to preach the gospel. America was in the throes of the Second Great Awakening, a revivalist movement that led to the formation of new religious denominations and fueled social reforms. By the early 1850s her unique voice was ringing out against injustice in meetings, lecture halls, and at women's suffrage conventions, and Sojourner Truth's place in history was secured.

Friends of the Slave

Among the abolitionists who took direct action to end slavery was a philanthropist from upstate New York, a committed Unitarian minister, and a rip-roaring man of means from the South.

☞ GERRIT SMITH:
Wealthy Eccentric

The son of Peter Smith, Sr., a partner of John Jacob Astor in the lucrative fur trade, Gerrit Smith would inherit a fortune that included more than a quarter-million acres of undeveloped land in New York and other states. Smith's riches enabled him to give generously to causes, such as women's suffrage, temperance,

Smith in the war years

prison reform and, most notably, the campaign to abolish slavery. In 1835 he helped fund the American Anti-Slavery Society and a year later began purchasing slaves so he could free them. He harbored others as they fled to Canada. Smith also served a term in Congress as a staunch antislavery advocate.

Smith's "Timbucto" In 1846 Gerrit Smith announced he would give 120,000 acres, which included the hamlet of North Elba, in the Adirondacks near Lake Placid, to 3,000 poor black people from New York. Smith thought the land could be cultivated to yield enough in cash crops to be worth $250, the amount needed in holdings to qualify to vote. The settlement was nicknamed Timbucto (sic) after a city in West Africa known for its celebration of racial and ethnic diversity.

A white settler named John Brown arrived in 1849 with his family in tow and, five years later, left to join his sons and attend to some business in Kansas (page 34).

The American Anti-Slavery Society Takes Shape

In 1833 William Lloyd Garrison, New York businessmen Arthur and Lewis Tappan, Rev. Theodore Dwight Weld, and black abolitionists, including Robert Purvis, founded the American Anti-Slavery Society (AASS), the first national organization of its kind. The goal was to convince whites in both the North and South of the inhumanity of slavery. One modus operandi was so-called moral suasion—changing hearts and minds by means of lectures and literature.

By 1840 the New York-based AASS boasted some 1,500 chapters around the country and well over 200,000 members. Then competing factions in the upper echelons split off to found their own organizations. One was the Tappan Brothers' American and Foreign Anti-Slavery Society. Another was James Birney's Liberty Party (page 60).

☛ THEODORE WELD: A Reverend's Shocking Tract

Connecticut-born Theodore Dwight Weld chose abolitionism and social reform over the church pulpit. His best-known act was compiling and distributing his *American Slavery as It Is: Testimony of a Thousand Witnesses*—a collection of slave-trading newspaper articles and advertisements gleaned from southern newspapers at the end of the 1830s. The tract, which also included rejoinders to proslavery arguments, was reprinted several times and helped turn the tide of public opinion. It also made a deep impression on Harriet Beecher Stowe as she began writing *Uncle Tom's Cabin*.

☛ CASSIUS M. CLAY: The "Lion of Whitehall"

The scion of one of the richest slaveholders in Kentucky, Cassius Clay became one of the most defiant and distinctive sons of the South. While at Yale, he was exposed to abolitionist thought and found William Lloyd Garrison's antislavery arguments as "water to a thirsty wayfarer." Clay kept his ties to northern abolitionists, and some historians suggest it was they who urged Clay to free his slaves—which he did, despite the typical Southern abolitionist's support for gradual, rather than immediate, emancipation.

Clay's Controversial Paper In 1845 Clay began publishing the abolitionist paper *True American,* which ensured he would no longer be elected to the Kentucky General Assembly (he served three terms). But desertion by voters paled next to the threat posed by anti-abolitionist mobs. Clay is said to have turned his office into a virtual bunker, and his skill in wielding a Bowie knife were legendary.

Whitehall—the grand estate of Clay, who lived to be 93 years old—has been restored as a Kentucky state historic site and welcomes visitors to glimpse the life of the man who came to be called the "Lion of Whitehall."

Alvin Coffey, Prospector

Alvin Coffey of Missouri wasn't the only slave who earned the money for his freedom in the California gold fields, but he was the first black inducted into the Society of California Pioneers.

Coffey's successful purchase of his freedom came after two tries and close to 10 years of prospecting. The first attempt, in 1849–1850, left him double-crossed by his owner, a Mr. Duvall, who had agreed to let Coffey go free for a thousand dollars' worth of gold. The second came three years after Duvall sold Coffey to Nelson Tindle (or Tindall) of Kansas City.

Armed with pick and shovel, Coffey earned more than enough to pay Tindle. Close friend Titus Hale takes up the story from there, quoted in *The Negro Trail Blazers of California* (1919): "[Coffey] then went to work to earn the money to pay for the freedom of his wife and daughters. After the arrival of his wife Coffey located in Red Bluff and opened a laundry. He also made a small fortune making hay at $16 per day, and in a few years was worth $10,000."

★ ★ ★ ★ ★ ★ ★ ★ ★ ★ ★ ★ THE CELEBRATED ★ ★ ★ ★ ★ ★ ★ ★ ★ ★ ★ ★

The Antebellum Political Landscape

The early republic was shaped by the Federalist Party championed by John Adams; it favored a strong central government. The Democratic-Republic Party supported by Thomas Jefferson envisioned a decentralized, agricultural society.

In the antebellum period the Republican Party would fade and reemerge in the image of the Federalists, while the Democratic Party would take many of its ideas from the Jeffersonians. The following nutshell descriptions present the relevant parties as they once were and orders them by the date they were formed.

Democratic Party Democrats favored local and regional control, and they opposed the rapidly increasing influence of banks, corporations, and industries. They also saw attempts to curb slavery as an attempt to destroy their way of life and take away their freedom. Jacksonian democracy, the legacy of the presidency of Andrew Jackson, favored expanding voting rights to all white men and involving the citizenry in government, and it flourished from the early 1830s to the 1850s.

Whig Party This party, which took its name from the British political party opposing undue royal authority, was formed in 1836 out of the National Republican Party to oppose Jeffersonian Democrats. The Whigs saw themselves as the party of the future. They believed in using the power of the federal government to promote banks, railroads, and industrialization. Social causes, such as temperance and free public schools, were also part of their vision.

Liberty Party This party resulted from a split in the American Anti-Slavery Society between political antislavery advocates and the Garrisonians—"moral suasion" advocates in league with William Lloyd Garrison. Political advocates James G. Birney and Gerrit Smith founded the party in 1840. The party had some successes at the local level, but in 1848 its members joined the coalition that became the Free Soil Party.

American (Know Nothing) Party In the 1830s and '40s a wave of antiforeigner sentiment swept the country as immigration brought increasing numbers of Catholic immigrants to America's Protestant shores. Conspiracy theories abounded: The Pope was plotting to move the Vatican to the Mississippi Valley; the Austrian monarchy was subsidizing Catholic immigration to gain control of the United States.

The secretive party earned its nickname because members answered, "I know nothing" when queried on party activities and membership. In 1854 the party scored big electoral victories in Massachusetts and the mid-Atlantic states. The members split over slavery in the following year, and most antislavery followers from the North joined the new Republican Party.

Free Soil Party Organized in Buffalo, New York, in 1848, this party was triggered by the Mexican War and the failed Wilmot Proviso, which stipulated that slavery would be barred from all lands acquired from a defeated Mexico. Likewise, the party opposed extending slavery into western territories. It promoted a homesteading law with the motto "Free Soil, Free Labor, Free Men." Its membership consisted of radical New York Democrats, Whigs, and former Liberty Party members.

Republican Party This party was formed in the wake of the Kansas-Nebraska Act (page 34) as a coalition of antislavery Whigs, Know Nothings, Free Soilers, and disaffected (and mostly northern) Democrats. It adopted the Free Soil Party's fierce opposition to the expansion of slavery, but tensions would remain between those who called for slavery's total abolition and those who did not. In 1860 the party would nominate Abraham Lincoln to run on a platform focused on halting the spread of slavery and preserving the Union.

THE
WAR
BETWEEN THE
STATES

1860–1865

The Mason-Dixon Line, named for two surveyors who helped resolve a territorial dispute, defined the eastern United States's North-South border—and by the late 1850s it had become a trembling fault line. The rumbles grew louder with the presidential election of Abraham Lincoln, who opposed the spread of slavery. The almost instant secession of seven slave states would lead to an all-out war, which erupted with the bombardment of Fort Sumter by soldiers defending the newly formed Confederate States of America.

This chapter is dedicated to the key battles and the Union and Confederate officers, soldiers, and sailors who fought them; intriguing sympathizers and spies on both sides; and the doctors, nurses, and ordinary citizens who came to the aid of the wounded and dying.

Bluecoats at the Cumberland Landing, Virginia, encampment

COMMANDERS IN CHIEF

In the country's 85th year of nationhood,
two men led a house divided. While both rose to the
occasion, only one would ultimately prevail.

———⇒≈《◎》≈⇐———

Seeds of Confrontation

While Lincoln wished to be president, Jefferson Davis took office only at the insistence of his compatriots. And quickly unfurling events would set these men on a collision course.

☛ THE RACE OF THE CENTURY

Abraham Lincoln and Illinois senator Stephen A. Douglas had faced off in a series of debates when running for the senate in 1858—Lincoln defending the exclusion of slavery in new territories, and Douglas promoting the right of citizens to vote on the question. Now, in 1860, the prize they sought was the presidency. Yet this would not be a two-party contest:

★ At the Democratic convention in Charleston, northern and southern delegates split over the inclusion of proslavery planks in the platform. Then, at a breakaway convention in Baltimore, southern Democrats nominated Kentuckian John C. Breckinridge, the sitting vice president under lame-duck president James Buchanan, as their candidate.

★ Another entrant was a former senator from Tennessee, John Bell, who represented the short-lived Constitutional Union party—ex-Whigs whose goal was to prevent disunion over slavery.

☞ THE LITTLE GIANT VS. THE LAWYER

Stephen Douglas, who stood 5'4" tall, was known as the "Little Giant" for good reason: He was a masterful politician and tactician. In the weeks leading up to the election, he broke with protocol and exhaustively stumped from state to state. From midsummer to November, Douglas presented himself as the one candidate who could keep a sectional divide at bay.

Lincoln, the only other true contender, took the more traditional tack and received supporters and information seekers at his Springfield law office. Meanwhile, his staff and supporters did the legwork.

The Wide-Awakes None of Lincoln's followers were more enthusiastic than the Wide-Awakes—uniformed young men who marched through the streets by torchlight and attracted people to rallies with free food and drink.

This grassroots movement had been born a couple of months before Lincoln was nominated, when he traveled to Hartford, Connecticut. He had been invited to city hall to address a meeting of supporters, most of whom were young and male—as was the meeting's leader: George C. Sill, Connecticut's 29-year-old lieutenant governor. The *New York Times* noted how Lincoln, "a man of the people," enthralled the Hartford audience with his "unpretending manner, conversational air…and dry humor."

Afterward, as Lincoln and Sill left to visit the mayor, young men thronged their carriage. Turning to Sill, Lincoln remarked, "The boys are wide awake. Suppose we call them the Wide-Awakes."

Hartford supporters formed a Wide-Awake marching club, and within weeks new clubs spread north and west. A month before the November election, a Wide-Awake march in Manhattan culminated with 12,000 people rallying at Union Square—the equivalent of 100,000-plus today.

☛ THE BIG DAY

Election day dawned on Tuesday, November 6, 1860. When the polls closed, Republican Lincoln and northern Democrat Douglas had received the lion's share of the almost 4,700,000 votes cast—Lincoln with about 490,000 more votes than Douglas. It was the electoral count that was lopsided: 180 for Lincoln, 72 for southern Democrat Breckinridge, and 39 for Constitutional Unionist Bell. Douglas won only Missouri and part of New Jersey—for an electoral grand total of 12.

Lincoln received no electoral votes in 10 of the slave states, and he wasn't even on the ballot in most—stark proof of a nation divided.

☛ SECESSION IN SHORT ORDER

As the election drew near, Southerners recoiled at the very thought of a Lincoln presidency. Rumors of slaves plotting to take up arms led to press reports of horrific incidents from Florida to Texas—stories that owed more to hysteria than truth.

Once news came that Lincoln would lead the nation, South Carolina took only 44 days to draw up and pass an ordinance of secession. Six more states followed suit—the last, Texas, on February 1, 1861. The nation split apart even before Lincoln took the oath of office.

Union Loyalists Even though 82 percent of southern legislators voted for secession, untold thousands of people were *not* in favor of seceding.

- ★ Though the South Carolina legislature voted unanimously to secede, 48 percent of Georgia's legislators and 38 percent of Alabama's voted "nay."

- ★ Virginia's northwestern counties were so against secession that eventually they were consolidated as the new state of West Virginia.

★ Union-loyal East Tennessee tried to secede from their new Confederate state, but the legislature quashed the effort; the area would later supply a steady stream of Union soldiers.

★ Counties in western North Carolina sought to remain as part of the Union, but to no avail.

Sam Houston: Texas's No. 1 Unionist

The historical figure most identified with Texas—Sam Houston, the victor over Santa Anna in the war for Texas independence, president of the Republic of Texas, and U.S. senator from the twenty-eighth state— was also his state's most high-profile Union loyalist. In 1859, as the winds of secession blew west, he ran as an Independent for governor.

The dashing, 6'2" Houston promised that, were he elected, "the Constitution and the Union embrace the principles by which I will govern."

And elected he was. Houston showed his famous backbone by delivering the inaugural address directly to the people from the steps of the capitol, not to the hostile legislators. "When Texas united her destiny with that of the United States," he declared, "she entered not into the North or South. Her connection was not sectional, but national."

King Cotton had made Texas very much a part of the South, and Governor Houston walked a tightrope to reconcile his unshakable anti-secessionist view with political realities. Still, when a popular vote overwhelmingly approved the ordinance of secession and the governor was called to the legislative chamber to swear allegiance of the Confederate States of America, he refused. The legislators promptly installed the lieutenant governor in his place.

Houston lived much of the two years that followed in the quiet, leafy town of Huntsville, a fierce Union loyalist until his dying day: July 26, 1863.

Jefferson Davis

☞ DAVIS RELUCTANTLY TAKES ON HIS TASK

Like many of his southern compatriots, Mississippi Senator Jefferson Davis believed the U.S. Constitution gave all states the right to leave the Union. But as armed conflict loomed, he spoke out for peace and compromise, in Congress and public venues north and south.

On January 21, 1861, Mississippi seceded, and Davis, in his resignation speech on the senate floor, said farewell to the Union. To no one's surprise, he also justified Mississippi's fateful step "on the basis that the states are sovereign." At another point, Davis explained why the principles of freedom and equality put forth by the Declaration of Independence "have no reference to the slave."

The Call to Command Returning home, Davis prepared to lead the Mississippi militia. Within two weeks, however, the Confederate Convention meeting in Montgomery, Alabama, named him provisional president of their fledgling confederacy—a position he accepted with regret and foreboding. When he read to his wife, Varina, the telegram informing him of his election, his tone was that of a man speaking "of a sentence of death."

☞ LAST-DITCH EFFORTS FOR PEACE

Virginians called for a Peace Convention in Washington, D.C., to discuss possible resolutions for the growing conflict. The congressmen and dignitaries who met on February 4, 1861 (the gathering was also called the "Old Gentlemen's Convention"), came from 14 northern states and 8 slave states. No one from the 7 slave states that had already seceded attended, most likely because on that very day, representatives in Montgomery,

Alabama, were forging a constitution for the new Confederate States of America (CSA) —a document that differed from the U.S. Constitution only in its empowerment of states' rights.

Senator John J. Crittenden of Kentucky issued the most prominent proposal at the Peace Convention. The Crittenden Compromise softened the Fugitive Slave Act of 1850 but also called for the admittance of new states whose constitutions allowed slavery. The last provision alone ensured that the Lincoln administration and the Republican-dominated Congress would reject the proposal.

☛ LINCOLN'S INAUGURAL ADDRESS

Given the stunning developments of the previous three months, the world waited with bated breath for Lincoln's March 4, 1861, inaugural address. True to character, Lincoln cut to the chase, stating that the "property and peace and personal security" of the people of the southern states would not be endangered by a Republican administration. He then repeated a quote from a previous speech: "I have no purpose, directly or indirectly, to interfere with the institution of slavery in the states where it exists. I believe I have no lawful right to do so."

He soon lay the potential for military action at the Confederacy's feet: "In your hands, my dissatisfied fellow countrymen, and not in mine, is the momentous issue of civil war. You can have no conflict without being yourselves the aggressors. You have no oath registered in heaven to destroy the government, while I shall have the most solemn one to preserve, protect, and defend it."

Our "Better Angels" William H. Seward, the new secretary of state, thought the first draft of the speech was a little too threatening to Southerners, so he suggested a more moderated and hopeful conclusion. Lincoln agreed, and gave the finale his unmatchable stamp:

"We are not enemies, but friends....The mystic chords of memory, stretching from every battlefield and patriot grave to every living heart and hearthstone, all over this broad land, will yet swell the chorus of the Union, when again touched, as surely they will be, by the better angels of our nature."

☛ THE QUESTION OF THE FORTS

Union forts in southern waters were part of the property Lincoln had pledged the Union would "hold and occupy." And both the North and South saw in one of them the opportunity to make political hay: Fort Sumter, the pentagon-shaped fort located offshore of Charleston—South Carolina's urban crown jewel.

Fort Sumter: The South's Catch-22 The question was whether Lincoln should reinforce or evacuate Fort Sumter, which was commanded by Maj. Robert A. Anderson. Major Anderson had sneaked his 80 soldiers to the empty—and more defensible—fort from neighboring Fort Moultrie in the wee hours of December 26, six days after South Carolina had passed its ordinance of secession.

After much hemming and hawing on the part of hawkish and dovish officials—among them three representatives sent to Charleston by Lincoln—the president-elect informed South Carolina governor Francis W. Pickens that "an attempt will be made to supply Fort Sumter with provisions only; and that, if such attempt be not resisted, no effort to throw in men, arms, or ammunition will be made…"

If Confederate soldiers attacked the supply ships, the South would be perceived as having started a war. If they did not, the Union would be seen as the winner in a battle of wills. Now the question was in the hands of Jefferson Davis—and on April 12, 1861, he would give the world his answer (page 75).

The Misses Todd, Taylor, and Howell

Mary Todd Lincoln and Varina Howell Davis gained worldwide renown. Jefferson Davis's first wife would no doubt be remembered, too, if she had not died young.

☞ MARY TODD LINCOLN: First Lady of the North

While Abraham Lincoln was doing chores on his father's Illinois farm, Mary Ann Todd of Lexington, Kentucky, was away at finishing school learning French and the social graces. Years later the two would meet in Springfield, Illinois, where the vivacious and witty Mary was enjoying an extended stay with her older sister Elizabeth Todd Edwards, a noted local hostess.

Lincoln and Todd married in 1842 and went on to have four sons, only one of whom lived to adulthood. Private letters reveal a strong and loving bond between husband and wife. But the public Mrs. Lincoln gained a reputation she would never shake: that of a woman who could be too sarcastic, too selfish, and too

Lincoln and his wife, Mary, are pictured with their two surviving sons: Robert Todd Lincoln, born in 1843, and Thomas "Tad" Lincoln, who was born in 1853 and died six years after his father's assassination.

rude. Her razor's-edge temper also led to more than one public (and publicized) display.

Mrs. Lincoln's Good Sides On the other side of the coin, Mrs. Lincoln was described as dignified, graceful, and cultured. She also was a good mother. One vacation with her sons was spent at the Equinox Inn, in Manchester, Vermont. In 1903 Robert Todd Lincoln, her only surviving son, later happened to buy land in Manchester and build Hildene, an estate now restored down to the last detail and open to the public.

☞ "KNOX" TAYLOR: The First Mrs. Davis

Jefferson Davis met the love of his life in 1832, when, as a commissioned officer, he was stationed at Fort Crawford in the Wisconsin territory. Sarah Knox Taylor, called "Knox" or "Knoxie," was the beautiful, educated daughter of Zachary Taylor, military commander of the installation and future president. Taylor, hoping to spare his daughter from the rigorous, often dangerous life of a military wife, disapproved. However, the courtship flourished.

Marriage and Tragedy Taylor's objections were finally overcome when Davis resigned from the army and planned to return to Mississippi to take up cotton farming. The couple married in a formal ceremony at Knox's aunt's house in Kentucky in June 1835.

Three months later Knox was dead at age 21, the victim of a malaria outbreak that nearly killed her husband as well. Davis recovered from the fever but not from the loss of his bride.

☞ VARINA HOWELL DAVIS: First Lady of the South

After the death of Knox, Jefferson Davis went into virtual seclusion for seven years. Even after emerging from his grief,

State of the Nations

The 1860 Census showed the demographic differences between northern states and the incipient Confederate States of America to be as wide as their respective ideologies—in large part because the North held a huge advantage in population, geographic size, and manufacturing. The economies of the Border States slanted northward.

The census counted almost everything households had to count, including horses and mules—individually. At the same time, the counting methods varied so widely that amounts were rough estimates at best—as in this chart, which compares manufacturing, agriculture, and one aspect of finance.

	North	Border States*	South
Population			
Whites	18,500,000	2,500,000	5,500,000
Free Blacks	210,000	120,000	130,000
Slaves		500,000	3,500,000
Economy			
Number of Factories	100,000	10,000	20,000
Manufactured Products Value	$1,500,000,000	$120,000,000	$155,000,000
Agricultural Labor Force**	2,000,000	360,000	700,000
Cash Value of Farms	$4,000,000,000	$700,000,000	$1,850,000,000
Bank Deposits	$190,000,000	$18,000,000	$47,000,000

*Delaware, Kentucky, Maryland, Missouri   ** Does not include slave labor*

he was interested only in his plantation and his books—until he met a tall, remarkably intelligent 17-year-old girl from Natchez, Mississippi.

Varina Howell was almost two decades younger than Davis and the child of ardent Whigs, though she agreed to accept Davis's southern Democratic politics as her own after their 1846 marriage. Above all, Varina knew she could never replace Knox in her husband's heart, but the realization did not discourage her.

Not Your Average Southern Belle Better educated and more outspoken than most young women, Varina was hardly the ideal southern belle—something of a liability throughout

the Davises' long marriage. For one thing, she had deep family roots in the North, where her grandfather Richard Howell twice served as governor of New Jersey. For another, she befriended a number of her northern relatives while at boarding school in Philadelphia. These northern connections later helped her settle comfortably into Washington's social life as the wife of a U.S. congressman from Mississippi.

CSA First Lady Varina Davis: social butterfly

Eyebrows Rise Initially, the cosmopolitan manners Mrs. Davis learned in the nation's capital served her well as First Lady in the Confederate capital of Richmond. But as the war dragged on, her public reputation would soon sink based on rumors of gross extravagance, elitism, insensitivity, and sympathy for the Union. True to her style, Varina soldiered on, undaunted and unbowed.

Officers and Gentlemen

Ulysses S. Grant and Robert E. Lee were joined in posterity by the likes of William T. Sherman, George McClellan, Stonewall Jackson, and Jeb Stuart. Lesser-known officers also played key roles as the Civil War progressed and, like their more famous counterparts, experienced highs and lows both military and personal.

<hr />

1861: Touch and Go

The war's first seven months began with the attack on Fort Sumter and the buildup of armies, progressed to a surprising Confederate victory at Bull Run (Manassas), saw Robert E. Lee struggle, and ended with the Union capture of an important southern port.

☛ MOMENT OF TRUTH AT FORT SUMTER

Tensions over Union-occupied Fort Sumter (page 70) had escalated after outgoing president James Buchanan dispatched the unarmed merchant ship *Star of the West* to Charleston to supply provisions and reinforce the fort with more men. Word spread southward, and as the ship entered Charleston harbor on January 9, 1861, gunfire from cadets at The Citadel, the state's military academy, drove the *Star of the West* out to sea.

Bombs Away On April 6 President Lincoln informed South Carolina governor Francis Pickens that provisions to Fort Sumter were forthcoming. In turn, Jefferson Davis ordered Brig. Gen. Pierre G. T. Beauregard—whom he had sent to command operations at Charleston Harbor—to get a jump on the arrival of Union ships and demand the evacuation of Fort Sumter.

Fort Sumter was the most impregnable of Charleston's military installations. This drawing shows an early Confederate flag.

Maj. Robert Anderson refused, and Beauregard's troops opened fire on the fort at 4:30 A.M. on April 12. Anderson's surrender came only after 34 hours of bombardment. The tragic upshot: fort captured, war in progress.

☛ SUMMONING THE TROOPS

The day after the attack on Fort Sumner, President Lincoln proclaimed the revolt in the South too powerful to be "suppressed by the ordinary course of judicial proceedings" and called for the states to enlist 75,000 militiamen for 90-day terms. The states easily fulfilled their quotas of soldiers, and volunteers made their way to Washington. By the end of the year, more calls would draw 700,000 soldiers serving three-year terms.

The initial raising of a northern army encouraged the secession of Virginia, Arkansas, North Carolina, and Tennessee, and in early March, Jefferson Davis called for the enlistment of

100,000 volunteers for one year. By January 1862 approximately 325,000 soldiers would be serving in the CSA Army.

States in the Balance The question was whether the four border states—all allowing slavery—would stay in the Union. The answer was an easy "yes" in Delaware, home to very few slaveholders. Maryland, Kentucky, and Missouri were less easily won over but came around in the end; nevertheless, between 30 and 40 percent of soldiers from these three states chose to fight for the Confederacy.

The First to Die

Among the first militias to answer Lincoln's call to Washington was the Sixth Massachusetts Regiment, mustered in the mill town of Lowell. On April 19, as the soldiers arrived in Baltimore by train and marched to another station, a mob of southern sympathizers lay in wait on Pratt Street. When the angry mob's stones turned to bullets, even the soldiers' 50-man-strong police escort was unable to protect four soldiers from lethal wounds.

The first to die in what became known as the Baltimore Riot was 17-year-old Luther Crawford Ladd, an Alexandria, New Hampshire, farmer's boy who had found work as a mechanic in Lowell. A drawing of Ladd accompanying a *Harper's Weekly* article titled "The First Victim of the War" showed him as a nice-looking young man obviously proud to be in uniform.

"All Hail to the Stars and Stripes!" In his *Life of Luther C. Ladd* (1862), Alexandria resident Kendrick Dickinson told how Private Ladd uttered "All hail to the stars and stripes!" with his dying breath—a phrase that soon gave rise to a popular song.

Ladd was not forgotten in Lowell, where the imposing Ladd-Whitney Monument honors the sacrifice of Ladd and fellow riot casualty Addison O. Whitney. Visitors to Ladd's hometown of Alexandria can view Ladd's grave at Crawford Cemetery and, across from the Alexandria town hall, the "capacious mansion" built by his father John Ladd, who went west to the gold fields and returned in "comfortable circumstances."

☛ LEE'S TERRIBLE DAYS OF DECISION

Returning to Washington in early March 1861, Robert E. Lee saw fellow officers resigning or being relieved of duty by commanders who mistrusted their loyalty. He continued to hope that Virginia would not secede and must have been buoyed when the first Virginia convention on secession rejected separation. His allegiance was strong when, near the end of March, he was promoted to full colonel and accepted command of a cavalry unit.

Stay or Leave? Then came Fort Sumter—and worse, Virginia's turnabout vote to secede. For several days and sleepless nights, Lee prowled the halls of his beloved Arlington and pondered his options. About 40 percent of officers from Virginia, including many men in Lee's family, stayed with the Union; others left the army and became neutral civilians. Lee left no record of his thoughts, but his wife, Mary, later called it the "severest struggle of his life." In the end, his devotion to Virginia prevailed.

☛ STATE OF THE ARMIES

In both the North and South, most men who answered the call to fight were civilians with little or no understanding of the discipline required to battle as a fighting-fit unit. Moreover, military rank had little meaning in small communities where soldiers were more likely to call an officer by his first name than "Captain."

Officers were often ill prepared as well. This was especially true of some of Lincoln's so-called political generals—men with no military experience but whose appointment would help secure the support for the war effort from Democrats, Irish and German immigrants, and other potential undecideds.

14ᵗʰ NY at Bull Run

Uneven Weaponry When it came to stocks of weaponry, the North had the clear advantage. The Confederacy had virtually no arms, so it seized what it could in southern arsenals. The imbalance was compensated in three ways:

★ The British, who relied on the South for cotton, sent arms to the Confederacy.

★ Factories—including the Tredegar Iron Works in Richmond and the College Hill Armory in Nashville, Tennessee—began or increased the manufacture of guns, swords, and cannons.

★ Rebel soldiers collected abandoned weaponry from battlefields after Yankee defeats or retreats.

*Confederate soldier
1862*

☛ BEN BUTLER'S "CONTRABAND"

In the spring of 1861, escaping slaves began seeking refuge at Union military facilities. Lacking legal authority to emancipate, the military had little recourse beyond returning escapees to their Southern masters. But Gen. Benjamin Butler (pages 92, 95), a brilliant criminal lawyer, declared refugees who turned up under his command at Fort Monroe, Virginia, to be "the contraband of war"—effectively ending their servitude.

Union officials quickly adopted Butler's policy, resulting in the liberation of tens of thousands of Southern slaves well ahead of the Emancipation Proclamation.

☛ REALITY CHECK AT BULL RUN (MANASSAS)

By summer, the first North-South test of strength was set to occur. The time: The mercilessly hot day of July 21. The place:

Bull Run Creek outside Manassas, Virginia, 28 miles south of Washington, D.C. The target: Rebel troops guarding a crucial railroad connection.

Both sides had much to prove:

★ The Union expected an easy victory that would show the folly of secession. Thirty-five thousand troops led by Maj. Gen. Irvin McDowell (page 99) would crush the Confederate troops, sever the rail link, and march triumphantly on to Richmond.

★ The Confederates aimed to show that their soldiers could outfight the industrialized North though sheer will and backwoods courage. Brig. Gen. P. G. T. Beauregard (page 94) oversaw 9,000 troops ensconced at Bull Run, and Jefferson Davis ordered Brig. Gen. Joseph E. Johnston to lead 20,000 more soldiers to the site.

Troop Colors—Green and Greener With their silken regimental flags of many colors fluttering in the wind, the Union militiamen marching south were a sight to behold. But they and their leader—Gen. Irvin McDowell were so woefully untrained that a march that should have taken one day took almost three.

The battle began before dawn, when McDowell fielded two exhausted divisions. The efforts of Union colonel William T. Sherman's brigade to strike at the Rebel right was slowed, and the Rebels rallied around Brig. Gen. Thomas J. Jackson's brigade and captured a vital hilltop.

With the afternoon arrival of the last of Gen. Joseph E. Johnston's troops, led by Kirby Smith, the Rebels forced the Yankees back. The combatants on both sides were green as grass, but it was the Union that went down in humiliating defeat.

☞ JOSEPH E. JOHNSTON: Yank to Reb

Joseph Eggleston Johnston, a judge's son who as brigadier general helped repel the Yankee assault at Bull Run, was raised in gentility in Abington, Virginia. He graduated from West Point in 1829, led combat forces in the Mexican War, and rose to quartermaster general of the U.S. Army. When Virginia seceded in May 1861, Johnston was the highest-ranked U.S. Army officer to resign and join the Confederacy.

The Johnston–Davis Feud In June, President Jefferson Davis promoted Johnston and four other men to full general, their priority gauged by the Confederate Congress according to class ranking at West Point, U.S. Army line officer rank, and other considerations. Johnston came in fourth, one step down from Robert E. Lee. Outraged, he fired off an angry letter to Jefferson Davis, and Davis replied in kind. Bad blood would remain between the two throughout the war and beyond.

Mixed Reviews Rank notwithstanding, Joe Johnston would go down in history as a one of the generals who won the South's first victory—at Bull Run (Manassas). He would also command both the Army of Northern Virginia and the Army of Tennessee. His critics, however, thought him too often reluctant to fight, and not without cause: His withdrawal of troops from the Peninsula, Atlanta, and Vicksburg campaigns earned him the nickname "Retreatin' Joe."

☞ THOMAS JONATHAN JACKSON: a.k.a. Stonewall

The Civil War's most famous nickname was bestowed in the heat of battle. During the fighting at Bull Run, Confederate general Barnard Bee's brigade was under heavy assault. Bee went directly

Stonewall Jackson

to Gen. Thomas J. Jackson for instructions. Jackson's terse and ambiguous reply: "Sir, we will give them the bayonet."

Bee, telling his officers that "Jackson stands like a stone wall," rallied his men behind Jackson's forces. Bee's exact meaning—whether admiration of Jackson's tenacious hold on a strategic position or frustration at his refusal to advance—remains a mystery. Bee was wounded and died the next day, leaving no further explanation. Jackson became "Stonewall," and his troops, the Stonewall Brigade.

> A former pupil recalled Jackson as the last man anyone expected to achieve greatness.

Other Telling Monikers Jackson's most striking feature was his deep blue-gray eyes, said to blaze in battle; his men called him "Old Blue Light." Before the war, as a professor at the Virginia Military Academy, he was a solemn know-it-all and hard disciplinarian generally disliked by his students. One student labeled Jackson an "automaton." A former pupil recalled Jackson as the last man anyone expected to achieve greatness.

☛ GEORGE B. McCLELLAN TAKES COMMAND

A product of both Philadelphia high society and West Point, George Brinton McClellan was short of stature but large in ego—and deservedly so. He marched Ohio volunteers to western Virginia in June and defeated small bands of Confederates trying to keep the locals from rejoining the Union—which they did in late November. His devoted soldiers dubbed him "Little Mac."

"A New and Strange Position" McClellan, now only 34 years old, had also distinguished himself in the Mexican War and as a railroad executive in Illinois and Ohio. With thousands of new troops flooding Washington after the Union debacle at Bull Run, Lincoln summoned McClellan to knock a ballooning and disorganized army into shape. The man who evolved from "Little Mac" to "Young Napoleon" was more than up to the job. As he wrote to his wife, Ellen, "I find myself in a new and strange position here: President, cabinet...all deferring to me. By some strange operation of magic, I seem to have become the power of the land."

☛ A NOT-SO-STELLAR START FOR "GRANNY LEE"

Having decided to join the Virginia forces, Robert E. Lee spent his early months as a Confederate general where he least wanted to be—behind a desk. His first venture into the field came in September, when he went into the mountains of western Virginia to advise Southerners attempting to cut off advancing Union forces under Gen. William S. Rosecrans.

The result was a debacle. His officers resented interference, and "Lee the Gentleman" was hesitant to assert authority. There

Lee as seasoned soldier

were skirmishes but no battles. Communications failed, and reconnaissance reporting was often wrong. Opportunities were squandered. Rosecrans's troops penetrated the mountains, and Lee went back to Richmond to face the music. His harshest critics dubbed him "Granny Lee" for his timorous leadership.

Lee the Engineer His next job was to fortify coastal defenses in South Carolina and Georgia. But this was engineering, not fighting. (Lee had requested and received assignment to the Engineering Corps when he graduated from West Point and, except for the Mexican War, had little battle experience.) Summoned back to Richmond, he returned to a desk as President Davis's special, though powerless, adviser. Yet through all the frustrations, "Granny Lee" was learning the leadership skills that shaped the General Lee who would finally take control of the war.

☛ A UNION WIN AT PORT ROYAL

President Lincoln had wasted no time in blockading southern ports (page 91) after the attack on Fort Sumter. The aim was to cripple the South's economy by keeping merchant ships from docking—a very tall order, given the Confederacy's well over 3,000 miles of coastline.

The Union Navy controlled only two Southern ports for use as bases—one in Virginia, the other in the Florida Keys. A third was seized on November 7, 1861, when a fleet of warships, coal and supply transports, and close to 13,000 sailors and marines arrived at Hilton Head, South Carolina. Four hours of expert land and sea maneuvers by Gen. Thomas W. Sherman and Rear Adm. Samuel F. DuPont led to the capture of Port Royal Sound—and with it two forts, several cotton plantations, and a blow to Confederate morale.

January–June 1862: Early Matches

The start of the first full calendar year of the war brought combat in the West as well as the East. Bloody battles in Tennessee signaled to the armies and the public that this would not be a short fight; the Union Navy captured New Orleans, and officers on both sides were met with wins and losses.

☞ THE WAR MOVES WEST

With a major South Carolina port now in Union hands (page 84), Lincoln and his generals began operations in the lower Mississippi Valley. Stationed at a Cairo, Illinois, Union Army supply base and training center was an obscure brigadier general named Ulysses S. Grant, whose troops had occupied the Confederate-friendly town of Paducah, Kentucky, in September 1861.

Grant's Bright Idea Gen. Henry Wager Halleck (page 130) oversaw the administration and training of Union troops in Missouri, Illinois, Arkansas, and western Kentucky. When Grant informed Halleck he believed he could open the Confederate-controlled Tennessee River by capturing Fort Henry—a likely pushover, given its waterlogged earthen construction and outdated guns—Halleck wavered. But he soon gave Grant the go-ahead, a decision he would not regret.

☞ THE TWO RIVERS CAMPAIGN

What became known as the Two Rivers Campaign began in West Tennessee on February 5, when Grant and Flag Officer Andrew H. Foote landed 15,000 troops within marching distance of Fort Henry, on the Tennessee River in the northwest corner of the state. Three wooden gunboats and four new ironclad gunners comprised their fleet.

When the boats arrived at the fort the next morning, commander Lloyd Tilghman saw the writing on the wall and ordered 2,500 of his men to march to Fort Donelson, 10 miles away on the Cumberland. Though the artillery force that stayed behind gave as good as it got and damaged the Union's supposedly invincible ironclads, it held out for only two hours before surrendering.

A Flotilla of Pook's Turtles

The ironclad gunboats built for Union western river operations were far superior to the steamships converted by the Confederate navy to the needs of war. They also couldn't have looked much odder.

Designed by naval architect Samuel F. Pook and built in the St. Louis shipyard of river engineer James B. Eads, the gunboats were wide, flat-bottomed, powered by a semi-protected paddlewheel, and sided by the sloping iron shell of the casemate—the chamber from which 13 guns poked. The casemate resembled a turtle shell, and the boats officially designated as City Class ironclads were soon nicknamed "Pook's Turtles." Seven of these gunboats would be built for the Western Flotilla as the war progressed. And as ingeniously designed as they were, the damage the boats sustained at Fort Donelson proved they were not fail-safe.

On December 12, 1862, the crew of the ironclad *Cairo* was clearing mines on the Yazoo River, north of Vicksburg, when an explosion tore a 12-foot hole in the hull. A century later, Civil War buffs and historians were gladdened when the *Cairo* was raised, restored, and put on display at Vicksburg National Military Park.

☛ ON TO FORT DONELSON

Grant's men now set out for Fort Donelson. In the meantime, soldiers from Bowling Green, Kentucky, under the command of Brig. Gen. John B. Floyd, were on their way to reinforce those manning the fort.

In the three-day battle that followed—with Albert Sidney Johnston, Nathan Bedford Forrest's cavalry, and others pitted against Union commanders, including John McClernand and Lew Wallace—the Confederates did their best. In the end, however, they realized the only way their soldiers could avoid capture was to flee to Nashville. A decision by Brig. Gen. Gideon Pillow to keep his exhausted soldiers in place resulted in the worst-case scenario: a Union victory, 15,000 Confederate casualties, and close to 13,000 men captured.

"Unconditional Surrender" Grant To save their own skin, Floyd (a former secretary of war and governor of Virginia) and Pillow (a lawyer) independently slinked off on separate skiffs. Left to surrender the fort and stand by his men was Brig. Gen. Simon B. Bolivar—himself a former governor, of Kentucky. He was also an old army friend of Grant's, so he suggested they discuss terms. Grant responded with "No terms except an unconditional and immediate surrender can be accepted."

Northerners rejoiced when they heard news of Grant's hard-nosed stand, and "Unconditional Surrender" Grant was born. Grant's act also did not escape the notice of Mr. Lincoln.

☛ DAVIS GETS REAL

In late February, the Confederate Congress elevated provisional president Jefferson Davis to official president. In his inaugural address, Davis summed up why southern states seceded after Lincoln's election:

> To save ourselves from a revolution which was about to place us under the despotism of numbers, and to preserve in spirit [and] form a system of government we believed to be peculiarly fitted to our condition, and full of promise for mankind, we determined to make a new association composed of States homogenous in interest, in policy, and in feeling.

An Early Verdict The Eleventh Edition of *Encyclopedia Britannica*, published in 1910, summoned the expressive prose of the time to encapsulate Commander in Chief Davis's strengths and weaknesses:

> *In the shortest time [Davis] organized and put into the field one of the finest bodies of soldiers of which history has record. Factories sprang up in a few months, supplying the army with arms and munitions of war, and the energy of the president was everywhere apparent. That he [also] committed serious errors, his warmest admirers will hardly deny. Unfortunately his admirable firmness developed into obstinacy, and exhibited itself in continued confidence in generals who were proved to be failures and in dislike of some of his ablest generals. He committed the great mistake, too, of directing the movement of distant armies from the seat of government, though those armies were under able generals. This naturally resulted in great dissatisfaction and more than once resulted in irreparable disaster.*

☛ McCLELLAN'S SLUGGISH START

George B. McClellan had been the toast of Washington after masterfully assembling the Army of the Potomac (page 82), but public and private acclaim soon grew stale. What, people asked in the winter of 1862, had kept him from taking his state-of-the-art forces to Richmond?

When McClellan finally moved in early March, he irked Lincoln by leading his army to the Virginia peninsula formed by the York and James rivers—not to the northern outskirts of Richmond, as Lincoln preferred. The president responded by relieving McClellan of his general-in-chief post but not, to the chagrin of many, of his leadership of the Potomac army.

Excuses, Excuses... When McClellan reached the area that would give his Peninsula Campaign its name, a successful month-long siege of Yorktown drove Confederate forces to Richmond. Then, from mid-April into late May, McClellan dawdled. On the one hand, the weather was terrible and Lincoln kept additional troops from McClellan in anticipation of a possible attack on Washington. On the other, McClellan believed the gross overestimate of Confederate troop strength cited by Allen Pinkerton, the oft-discredited head of his secret service.

When McClellan yet again failed to get a move on after Antietam (page 102), Lincoln would yet again demote him, this time relieving him of leadership of the Potomac Army.

☛ SHENANDOAH: Stonewall's Shining Moment

From March 23 to mid-June, as Union forces were gearing up to strike Richmond, Stonewall Jackson and 4,200 soldiers were assigned to protect the Confederate-held Shenandoah Valley. This 140-mile-long valley separating the Blue Ridge and Appalachian Mountains was a vital agricultural region and also provided a direct north-south passage.

Hit and Run Jackson's first attack, against forces led by Union Maj. Gen. Nathaniel P. Banks at Kernstown, failed. The news frightened President Lincoln and General McClellan, who—not surprisingly—overestimated Jackson's strength and shifted Union troops to the valley to prevent a Confederate surge northward.

Jackson's reinforced corps of 17,000 men moved up and down the mountains with speed and stealth. From McDowell and Winchester to Port Republic, he won battles and skirmishes and then disappeared before the smoke cleared. This hit-and-run tactic drew tens of thousands of Union troops deeper into the valley and farther from McClellan's army.

☛ THE BATTLE OF SHILOH

After Grant's success on the Tennessee and Cumberland rivers, Gen. Albert Sidney Johnston, the Confederate commander in the West, evacuated his forces from Nashville in late March. His destination was Corinth, Mississippi, the crossroads of the Memphis & Charleston and Mobile & Ohio railroads and the western Confederacy's most important railroad junction. Brig. Gen. P. G. T. Beauregard, leading troops down from the garrison in Columbus, Kentucky, joined him there.

Grant at Pittsburgh Landing Grant, ordered by Halleck to seize the junction, moved up the Tennessee River with just over 40,000 men and stopped to spend the night in a peach orchard at Pittsburgh Landing, 22 miles north of Corinth. Meanwhile, 25,000 soldiers from Maj. Gen. Don Carlos Buell's Army of the Ohio were marching down from Nashville.

Initial Shock and Awe A golden opportunity stared General Johnston in the face—a surprise attack on Grant's army before Buell and his men could arrive. On the morning of April 6, he grabbed it.

Wave after wave of Rebels overwhelmed Union forces commanded by the likes of William T. Sherman and John A. McClernand, who battled as best they could and rallied briefly near tiny Shiloh Church. But the Confederacy prevailed. At around 5:30 P.M., Beauregard wired Jefferson Davis and reported a complete victory.

A Quick Turnaround Troops led by Buell and Lew Wallace (the latter from their camp 10 miles upriver) arrived that evening—truly a case of better late than never. With Grant's army thousands of men stronger, the tide changed like a tidal wave on day two. In fact, by mid-afternoon Beauregard had to admit defeat and retreat to Corinth.

Grant would have pursued the retreating troops if his own had not been severely battered. Total casualties at the Battle of Shiloh equaled those at Waterloo (the battle that dethroned Napoleon I), and Americans knew they were in for a long and bloody fight.

☞ THE RETRIEVAL OF FORT PULASKI

After the attack on Fort Sumter, three Georgia infantries seized the main defense guarding the important port of Savannah, Georgia—Fort Pulaski. Now, in early 1862, the Union wanted it back.

The Anaconda Plan This operation was in accordance with the plan proposed by the aged Gen. Winfield Scott, hero of the War of 1812 and the Mexican War: the blockading of ports on the Atlantic and Gulf coasts and military control of the Mississippi River. The press dubbed Scott's idea the Anaconda Plan, after the snake that kills its prey by constriction.

Early on the morning of April 10, a U.S. Army expedition that had established itself on nearby Tybee Island began to bombard Fort Pulaski after its commander, the overconfident Col. Charles A. Olmstead, refused to surrender. Pulaski was a so-called third-system fort—a defense with stone walls so thick it was thought invincible. But the newfangled rifled artillery was proving otherwise.

White-Flag Time Riflemen led by Quincy A. Gillmore, a captain who had been brevetted to brigadier general, blasted a hole in the southeast corner of the fort and kept at it until the wall was breached. At 2:30 in the afternoon, Colonel Olmstead replaced the Confederate flag with the white flag of surrender. The Union had not only ensured that Savannah was no longer a safe port for Confederate blockade runners but also that goliath stone forts were obsolete.

☞ FARRAGUT TAKES NEW ORLEANS

In the spring of 1862, the port of New Orleans was ripe for picking off—the prize plum of the Union's Anaconda Plan (page 91). And it fell to Flag Officer David Farragut of the U.S. Navy.

Between April 18 and 25, Union boats commanded by Farragut and naval officer David D. Porter bombarded two forts and the Confederate fleet to open the path to New Orleans. They succeeded, and on his arrival, Farragut demanded the city's surrender in the face of angry crowds.

A silly "who surrenders first" dispute between Mayor John T. Monroe and Maj. Gen. Mansfield Lovell (the Confederate commanding officer) dragged on for four days, so Farragut sent a group of marines to raise the American flag over two public buildings.

Enter Benjamin Butler Two days later Maj. Gen. Benjamin Butler (page 79) took control, immediately declaring martial law to calm the riotous city. New Orleans benefited from many of his orders, particularly a massive cleanup that almost eliminated yellow fever, but the local elite despised his zero-tolerance policies, harsh punishments, and help for the poor at the expense of the wealthy.

Irked New Orleans ladies

How to Offend a Lady When women of high social standing began openly harassing Union soldiers—one emptied a chamber pot over Flag Officer Farragut—Butler issued General Order No. 28, specifying that "any female" who "shall…insult or show contempt" for Union soldiers be treated as "a woman of the town plying her avocation." This threat of arrest for common prostitution ended the protests and prevented a likely escalation to violence. It also earned Butler the nickname "The Beast."

And Europe, Too As news of Butler's order spread, it was widely misrepresented as a license for physical assault, causing outrage in neutral Europe. Fearful of an English or French alliance with the Confederacy, Lincoln replaced the contentious Butler with the younger (and gentler) Nathaniel P. Banks.

☞ LEE TO THE FRONT

Back in the Eastern Theater, George B. McClellan continued to inch toward Richmond, despite Stonewall Jackson's immobilization of 50,000-plus Union soldiers in the Shenandoah Valley. McClellan would have to cross the flooded Chickahominy River to reach Fair Oaks, Virginia (about 20 miles northwest of Richmond), where his troops would join those on the opposite bank.

Joe Johnston's Chance Confederate general Joseph E. Johnston (page 81), now head of the Army of Northern Virginia, saw his chance to strike. His plan was for 23 Rebel brigades to descend on Fair Oaks and force the Yankees into the river.

The battle of Seven Pines began on the afternoon of May 31. At Johnston's headquarters sat Robert E. Lee, still little more than Jefferson Davis's adviser. And who should show up but the micromanaging Davis himself? The two men were almost caught in the crossfire as they rode out to observe the fighting.

Jeff Davis's Decision As night fell, a badly wounded General Johnston was one of the casualties brought into Fair Oaks. With Johnston out of commission, Davis asked Lee to take over the Army of Northern Virginia—and the man of honor from Arlington would command this most famous of Confederate armies to the end.

☛ LEE'S CRUCIAL SEVEN DAYS

Lee immediately sprung into action. He increased the Army of Northern Virginia's strength to 85,000 and dispatched Brig. Gen. Jeb Stuart on a reconnaissance mission that took him all the way around Union encampments. Lee then prepared to fight what would be called the Seven Days Battles.

Battles or skirmishes at Mechanicsville, Gaines' Mill, Savage's Station, Malvern Hill, and other sites combined to leave General McClellan's army crippled to the point of inaction. For now, Richmond was out of the grasp of President Lincoln and the Union Army, and Gen. Robert E. Lee was the Confederacy's last best hope.

———— ((◉)) ————

The Men in Charge, Part 1

Sherman…Jackson…Farragut…Some Civil War officers' names still resound, but others are less familiar. Regardless, they were well known in the war era, whether they succeeded militarily, failed miserably, or fell somewhere in between.*

☛ P. G. T. BEAUREGARD (CSA): Cosmopolitan Creole

A Louisianan of Spanish and Creole ancestry, Pierre Gustave Toutant Beauregard was born on a sugar plantation near New Orleans. The worldly, talkative Beauregard didn't shy away from self-promotion and even ghostwrote his own biography. There was much to tell: Few, if any, Confederate generals saw more action from the start of the war to the finish. Beauregard scholars describe the general as one of the most colorful and romantic figures of the era.

*In the alphabetically ordered profiles that follow, Union generals are designated as (USA), and those of the Confederate States of America as (CSA).

Beauregard's Smashing Debut

When Louisiana seceded, Beauregard jumped into military service feetfirst as the commander of the Confederate forces guarding Charleston Harbor—and, in turn, attacking Fort Sumter. Before 1861 was out, Brigadier General Beauregard had commanded the victorious forces at the battles of Shiloh and Corinth, Mississippi. In 1863 he would return to Charleston and defend it from Union naval and land forays.

Pierre G. T. Beauregard

☞ BENJAMIN BUTLER (USA): More Than Met the Eye

Ben Butler was no beauty. But beyond his portly physique and one crossed eye was a prodigious intelligence. This self-taught attorney's legal skills and courtroom theatrics led to a long political career and eventually a command position as one of Lincoln's political generals (page 78). He won the president's gratitude by quelling the Baltimore Riot of April 1861, but he usually served best as an administrator. After the Civil War's end, he would side with the Radical Republicans as a U.S. Congressman.

Ben's Path Born in New Hampshire, Benjamin Franklin Butler spent his youth in the Massachusetts mill town of Lowell. There he developed a lifelong intolerance of rich plutocrats who earned wealth and power on the backs of the working class.

Butler had little contact with blacks, however, until he realized he had to decide how to deal with runaway slaves at his post in Virginia (page 79). The war—along with his command of Union troops occupying New Orleans (page 92)—transformed Butler into a champion of universal equality, and during Reconstruction he would spearhead passage of the Ku Klux Klan Act of 1871 and the Civil Rights Act of 1875.

☛ WILLIAM T. SHERMAN (USA): Modern Soldier

William "Cump" Sherman

William Tecumseh Sherman was born on February 8, 1820, in Lancaster, Ohio. His father, Judge Charles R. Sherman, chose the newborn's middle name to honor the great chief whose people, the Shawnee, were native to Ohio. Though a native Ohioan himself, Judge Sherman's deep American roots went back to the arrival of Englishman Edmond Sherman to the Massachusetts Bay Colony in 1634.

The redheaded boy nicknamed Cump was said to be "the smartest" of 11 Sherman children. After an illness killed his father in 1829 and his widowed mother fell on hard times, he was taken in by the family of attorney Thomas Ewing, a future U.S. Senator from Ohio. At age 16, Sherman was off to West Point, and three years later graduated near the head of his class.

Attuned to the Times Service in the Mexican War, banking in California, and supervision of the Louisiana State Seminary & Military Academy (later Louisiana State University) followed. Sherman left Louisiana in the early days of secession and joined the army as a colonel. Science and invention was changing the face of war, and no one grasped this better than the intellectual and curious Sherman.

Sherman and Grant Sherman also knew whom to befriend. After providing logistical support for Ulysses S. Grant's capture of Fort Donelson, he wrote Grant and volunteered for military service. As a result, he was made commander of the 5th Division of the Army of West Tennessee on March 1, 1861. A few weeks later, at the Battle of Shiloh, Sherman's actions would be critical to the Union's ultimate victory.

☛ NATHAN B. FORREST (CSA): "The Wizard of the Saddle"

One of the South's most storied commanders, Nathan Bedford Forrest was feared, revered, and eventually reviled. Born dirt poor in rural Tennessee, Forrest had become a wealthy slave trader by the time the war began. A tall, dashing horseman with rare courage, a quick temper, and a genius for strategy, Forrest entered the army a private and departed a lieutenant general.

Devil, Too? Unlike other Confederate officers, many of whom were by-the-book West Pointers, Forrest followed his gut and had a combat style of his own. Dubbed the "Wizard of the Saddle," he foiled Union forces with his speed, surprise attacks, and audacious bluffing. Gen. William T. Sherman went so far as to call him a "devil" who should be destroyed at all costs.

☛ DAVID G. FARRAGUT (USA): America's First Admiral

David Glasgow Farragut's merchant sea-captain father was born in Minorca, Spain, and emigrated to fight in the Revolutionary War. He married a North Carolinian named Elizabeth Shine, and David was born in East Tennessee in 1801. The Farragut family moved to New Orleans six years later, and all was well until Elizabeth became ill and died. David was taken into the home of David Porter, Jr., a rising naval star whose seaman father had been a friend of Jorge Farragut.

Rear Adm. David G. Farragut

The Four-Foot-Tall Midshipman Obsessed with ships from his earliest days, David was able to join the navy in 1810. At age 12, he took the wheel to dock a ship captured in the War of 1812. A career as a sea captain followed, and when the Civil

War broke out, Farragut chose to side with the Union despite his Southern birth and upbringing.

Farragut's capture of New Orleans was undeniably a feather in his naval cap, but it would be his 1864 "Damn the torpedoes!" victory at Mobile Bay (page 134) that would make him the first U.S. Navy admiral.

☛ EARL VAN DORN (CSA): Creative Soul, Weak Commander

Earl Van Dorn was a proficient poet and painter. But as commander of the Army of the West in the Trans-Mississippi Theater, the Mississippi-born brigadier general fell short. In March 1862 he fought the Battle of Pea Ridge, Arkansas, with a numerically superior but ill-equipped force and suffered a thumping defeat securing Missouri for the Union. Van Dorn would redeem himself only as a cavalry commander for the Army of Tennessee. In one success he captured 1,500 of Grant's Vicksburg Campaign soldiers at Holly Springs, Mississippi, and destroyed tons of Union supplies.

A Pulp Fiction End Van Dorn never met a Southern Belle he didn't like, and his womanizing cost him his life. One dalliance was with a doctor's wife named Jessie Peters. In May 1863 Jessie's wronged husband walked into Van Dorn's headquarters in Spring Hill, Tennessee, stole up behind him, and shot him in the back of the head—and Van Dorn went the way of all flesh at age 43.

☛ BRAXTON BRAGG (CSA): Equal Opportunity Offender

Were it not for Braxton Bragg's daring rescue of Jefferson Davis during a Mexican War battle, Bragg might not have risen as high as he did. Simply put, he was not a nice guy. The argumentative North Carolinian was as abrasive and rude to superiors in the Army of the Tennesee as he was to underlings.

Strict But Lax On the plus side, the man who was one of seven generals in the Confederacy (he was promoted after the

Battle of Shiloh) was a strict disciplinarian. But he was much better at planning than execution. He also sometimes failed to press a military advantage and finish the job—as was the case at the Battle of Perryville, fought during Bragg's campaign to lure Kentucky back to the Confederacy.

Gen. Braxton Bragg

Calls to remove Bragg from his post were numerous, but Jefferson Davis continued to stand by his man. After Bragg's poor performance at the Battle of Chattanooga, even he knew he should leave. Davis accepted Bragg's resignation, but he kept him in the army as an adviser.

☛ IRVIN McDOWELL (USA): Double Whammy at Bull Run

Ohio-born Irvin McDowell taught military tactics at West Point, his alma mater. And it has been said that the academic tactics he devised at First Bull Run (page 79) were too complex for his raw troops and cost the Union its expected win.

To be fair, McDowell was a political general, having been touted by Secretary of the Treasury Salmon P. Chase. Furthermore, it was politicians who pushed for the premature offense against Confederate troops at Bull Run.

Serious Déjà Vu McDowell carried on and was brevetted a major general after an August 1862 victory at Cedar Mountain, Virginia. But a replay at Bull Run (page 100) ruined his career. A communications mix-up during battle was pinned on McDowell, and a court of inquiry blamed him for the Union's loss. He was later cleared.

Exonerated or not, McDowell was consigned to a desk job in the Department of the Pacific. He spent his later years as San Francisco's Parks Commissioner, no doubt more than concerned with baseball and footraces than things military.

July–December 1862: Advantage Rebels?

After the Confederate success in the Seven Days battles, the Rebels once again knocked down the Yankees at Bull Run. Lee's subsequent push toward Union territory was stopped by a bloody face-off at Antietam but was followed by a decisive victory at Fredericksburg. Meanwhile, Lincoln prepared to free the slaves.

☛ BULL RUN REDUX

Fresh from victory, Lee's next target was the Army of Virginia, a short-lived consolidation of disjointed northern Virginia troops whose purpose was to guard Washington, D.C., and the Shenandoah. The army's commander was Kentuckian John Pope, who had developed a reputation for haughtiness and self-promotion. A few months earlier, Pope had headed the Army of the Mississippi and won kudos when he captured 7,000 Rebel soldiers at Island No. 10 and opened the river down to Fort Pillow.

Pope Flubs It In late August, Stonewall Jackson's corps destroyed the Army of Virginia's supply base at Manassas and drew Pope like a moth to the flame. The fighting on the first day Second Bull Run ended in a draw. The next-day arrival of CSA general James Longstreet's reinforcements somehow escaped Pope's notice, and a massive Rebel assault resulted in almost five times the casualties of First Bull Run. Pope retreated and then pinned the blame on anyone but himself—and though he would stay in the Union Army, his star had fallen for good. The battle was also a blow to Irvin McDowell (page 99), who had lost the first battle of Bull Run.

☛ LINCOLN ON THE ROPES

In the summer of 1862, President Lincoln was in terrible shape. With the Rebels still active in the East and West, no end to the war was in sight. England, France, and Russia were on the verge of recognizing the Confederacy's nationhood, largely because shortages of Southern cotton caused European unemployment to rise. Abolitionists won more hearts and minds and strengthened their case for immediate emancipation of the slaves—more of whom became "freed" contraband with each Union win.

The Slavery Issue Since May, Lincoln had been thinking slavery was not only a matter of principle but of policy. Then, on July 17, Congress passed the First Confiscation Act, which furthered the move toward emancipation by identifying the Confederates as traitors and legalizing the confiscation of their property—slaves included.

Lincoln signed the act, but its ambiguities troubled him. He and Secretary of State William Seward agreed that clear-cut emancipation could come only with an executive order. Yet that order would have to wait until the Union had a victory; otherwise, it could be seen, in Seward's words, "as the last measure of an exhausted government, a cry for help."

The question was *when* a victory would roll in. The good-enough answer came in September, at Antietam.

☛ ANTIETAM: A Critical Clash

Robert E. Lee knew his army couldn't breach Washington's defenses, so he targeted Harrisburg, Pennsylvania, the Union's main railroad and bridge links to the West. On September 15 he got word that Stonewall Jackson expected to capture the Union Army supply base at Harpers Ferry—so Lee chose to send the whole Army of Northern Virginia to nearby Sharpsburg, Maryland, a mile past the Potomac and one step closer to Pennsylvania.

Draw or Not? When George B. McClellan caught up with Lee near Sharpsburg, his forces outnumbered Lee's two to one. The battle at Antietam Creek began at dawn the next day, when

Lincoln visited the Antietam battlefield 10 days after the smoke cleared.

Union general Joseph's Hooker's corps delivered a powerful punch to Lee's left flank. More punches and counterpunches followed, and the three-day battle ended in a draw.

In the larger sense, Antietam was a vital win for the Union. Lee's invasion of northern territory failed, and he retreated across the Potomac; England and France pulled back from recognizing the Confederate States of America; and Lincoln had the "victory" he needed to justify freeing the slaves.

Deadly Score On the fields of battle at Antietam lay some 26,000 dead or wounded Union and Confederate soldiers— roughly three times the casualties suffered by U.S. and U.K. World War II forces during the D-Day invasion of Normandy.

☞ McCLELLAN GETS BOOTED FOR GOOD

After Antietam, Henry Halleck ordered McClellan to cross the Potomac and march to Richmond. But the finicky general said he couldn't comply until his army was once again shipshape.

The press ridiculed McClellan, and Lincoln did not conceal his ire. On October 26 Little Mac began to move his army—but with so little urgency that Robert E. Lee was able to call on Richmond. On November 7 Lincoln chose Maj. Gen. Ambrose Burnside over McClellan to lead the Army of the Potomac.

Clothes Made the Man?

In many respects, army regulations of the Civil War era were lax by today's standards. Accordingly, uniforms weren't always uniform, and two officers in particular were noted for their individualistic attire.

★ **Jeb Stuart** The look affected by Jeb Stuart (page 107), Robert E. Lee's chief cavalryman, harked back to the early colonial Virginia cavaliers (originally, gentlemen horsemen loyal to the British crown), long beard and all. His outfit included a wide-brimmed, ostrich-plumed hat; a black cape with red silk lining; gauntlets (gloves); and jackboots, glossy leather boots extending above the knee. How often Stuart bothered to don all items at once is open to question.

★ **George Armstrong Custer** The Union officer who became famous after his last stand at Little Big Horn first gained his reputation for daring in the Peninsula Campaign and at Gettysburg. He showed off as a dresser as well, from his curly locks down to his carefully polished boots. Custer's clothing items of choice included a red neckerchief, a black velveteen vest, and crisp white shirts. A frequent finishing touch was a dash of cologne or perfumed oil.

☛ UNION DISASTER AT FREDERICKSBURG

In late November the Army of the Potomac, with Ambrose Burnside now in charge, arrived at the Rappahannock River, a notoriously difficult barrier for Union troops because of its lack of fords and bridges. The army had ordered pontoons that would bridge the river at Fredericksburg, but the War Department had yet to deliver. The delay allowed Robert E. Lee to position 75,000 soldiers in the hills above the city.

A Fatal Decision The pontoons finally arrived, and on December 11, in the dark of night, army engineers began installing them. With dawn, what began as sniping from Confederate militias in the town center escalated to battle when Union soldiers crossed the river in boats, fought the Rebels in the streets, and occupied the town.

Now the question was whether to charge up into the hills to engage Lee's army. Against all advice, Burnside assigned regiments to do just that, and wave after wave of Union soldiers fell in some of the worst carnage of the war.

Emancipation Is Proclaimed

President Lincoln had gravitated from a belief in gradual emancipation of the slaves to a serous flirtation with colonization (he was quoted as saying that colonization could "[free] our land from the dangerous presence of slavery" and "restore a captive people to their long-lost fatherland"). Now, in the late summer of 1862, he saw immediate emancipation as the solution. But detractors like Horace Greeley, editor of the *New York Tribune,* had no way of knowing.

Lincoln's Lead-Up On August 20 Greeley published a lengthy editorial titled "The Prayer of Twenty Millions," which took Lincoln to task for his slowness to act. The president's response, published two days later, was designed to garner popular support for the impending proclamation by covering all the bases. An excerpt:

> *My paramount object in this struggle is to save the Union, and is not either to save or to destroy slavery. If I could save the Union without freeing any slave I would do it, and if I could save it by freeing all the slaves I would do it; and if I could save it by freeing some and leaving others alone I would also do that.*

"Forever Free" On September 22 Lincoln issued the Preliminary Emancipation Proclamation, which stated that on January 1, 1863, "all persons held as slaves, within any state…shall be then, thenceforward, forever free." Voices everywhere rang out in jubilation or fury, and the world kept turning on its axis.

Men in Charge, Part 2

Two Union generals who were famous in their day are less remembered than a Confederate general named Longstreet, who,
rightly or wrongly, came to represent failure. The war's leaders
also included a first-generation Irish American from upstate New
York and a superior horseman born on a Virginia plantation.

☞ GEORGE H. THOMAS (USA): The Rock

In today's parlance, West Pointer George Henry Thomas—a
Virginian from a slaveholding family—was a mature-age student.
He waited until he was 20 to enter the academy, the reason
cadets called him Old Tom. When the Civil War began almost
three decades later, the Yanks among them (including Thomas's
ex-roommate William T. Sherman) no doubt cheered his decision to side with the Union.

Success in the West Thomas played a major role in the
Union's Tennessee campaigns, starting at Stones River. In September 1863 he would hit the heights as commander of the Army
of the Cumberland's 14th Corps at the Battle of Chickamauga;
his refusal to retreat made him "the Rock of Chickamauga"—a
nickname that stuck. But the Rock did anything but stand still.
As full commander of the Army of the Cumberland, he would
pummel the Rebels in Chattanooga and Nashville (pages 123,
136), thanks to his masterful direction of the cavalry.

☞ JOSHUA L. CHAMBERLAIN (USA): The Professor

The future brigadier general who fought at Chancellorsville and
would become famous at Gettysburg was an unlikely volunteer
when he took up the Union cause. He had studied Latin and
Greek in the attic of his parents' farmhouse outside Brewer,
Maine, to meet the entrance requirements of Bowdoin College—

where he not only graduated but became an esteemed professor. At his alma mater he mastered 10 languages and taught a variety of subjects to students not much younger than himself.

Fight and Repeat The dashing Chamberlain, with his noble forehead and massive mustache, joined the new 20th Maine Volunteers in August 1862. Combat at Fredericksburg was followed by his appointment as colonel of the Maine 20th and its triumph at Gettysburg's Little Round Top (page 118).

During the months-long siege of Petersburg, Chamberlain was almost left for dead during a battle fought in June 1864, but he kept coming back for more. In fact, by the war's end he had fought in well over 20 battles and skirmishes, was cited for bravery four times, and suffered numerous wounds.

☛ JAMES LONGSTREET (CSA): Man Down

Raised in Georgia, James Longstreet was of Old Dutch stock (his ancestor Dirck Langestraet settled in the Dutch colony of New Netherland in 1657). As the son of successful cotton planters, James was admitted to West Point. He graduated near the bottom of his class, but he got along well with the cadets—among them

James Longstreet

Ulysses S. Grant and George H. Thomas.

Longstreet's Confederate Army service began at First Bull Run, where his performance led to a promotion from lieutenant general to major general. But he was stopped dead by personal tragedy in early 1862, when three of his four children succumbed to scarlet fever. Recovery gradually came with successes at the battles of Seven Days, Antietam, and Fredericksburg.

War Horse to Scapegoat Gettysburg was another matter. As commander of the 1st Corps of the Army of Northern Virginia, Longstreet made tactical decisions that estranged him from Robert E. Lee (who had fondly called him his "Old War Horse). This and his supposed oversight of the ill-fated Pickett's Charge at Gettysburg made him history's scapegoat for a defeat that would rock the Confederacy.

☛ PHILIP SHERIDAN (USA): "Little Phil"

Philip Henry Sheridan

If Philip Sheridan was short (he stood 5' 5") he looms large in Civil War lore. Many historians rank him as one of the top Union generals, up there with Grant and Lee. He had a knack for deploying men and supplies in just the right measure, and treated his soldiers with the utmost respect. "Put your faith in the common solider," he said more than once, "and he'll never let you down."

Fast Learner Sheridan, who was born in upstate New York, began his fast-track rise as a staff officer for Maj. General Henry Halleck. He first fought as colonel of the 2nd Michigan Cavalry at Booneville, Mississippi, and earned a promotion to brigadier general. Action at Stones River in early 1863 brought a promotion to major general.

In 1864 Sheridan became known for his scorched earth mission in the Shenandoah—his cavalry's seizure of livestock and the destruction of factories, railroads, mills, and barns. Virginians called it "The Burning," and it foreshadowed Sherman's March to the Sea. The man who treated his soldiers so well was hard as nails when it came to the enemy.

☛ JEB STUART (CSA): "The Eyes of Lee's Army"

James (Jeb) Ewell Brown Stuart was born on a Virginia plantation and graduated from West Point in 1854, exactly a quarter of a century after Robert E. Lee. The cadet was noted for his horsemanship—a talent that would not only make him Lee's top cavalryman but also a peerless intelligence gatherer.

Ambitious and showy, Stuart set himself apart with his cavalier's plumed hat. But substance trumped style in battle after battle: Seven Days, Second Bull Run, Antietam, Fredericksburg, Chancellorsville (where, on the mortal wounding of Stonewall Jackson, he took command of his friend's 28,000-man Second Corps), Gettysburg, and Wilderness.

One Last Charge Stuart's brilliant career ended in a skirmish during General Grant's Overland Campaign. On May 11, 1864, at Yellow Tavern—an abandoned inn six miles north of Richmond—Stuart raced to repel a charge by Yankee horsemen and was wounded by the last of 12 shots fired at close range. He died the next day, six weeks after his 31st birthday.

Col. Dixon Miles, Sot

Dixon Stansbury Miles, of Maryland and West Point, got off on the wrong foot in the war. He was forced to take a months-long leave of absence after being proved drunk at First Bull Run, where he was in command of Union troops that (luckily) weren't called into action.

September 1862 found Miles in charge of the federal arsenal at Harpers Ferry. Gen. Henry Halleck instructed Miles to defend the town from Stonewall Jackson's forces until General McClellan's army arrived. But Miles left some of the heights above the town unmanned and made it easy for Jackson to swoop in. Miles conferred with his brigade commanders and decided to surrender.

The surrender of 12,419 men would be the largest until World War II, and the court of inquiry that looked into it called Miles inept almost to the point of "imbecility." It also found Miles had been drunk yet again.

In those days, alcoholism was considered a character defect, and Miles went to his grave in disgrace. He never knew it, however: As he prepared to surrender, shrapnel from an exploding shell pierced his leg—a wound that killed him a day later.

★ ★ ★ ★ ★ ★ ★ ★ ★ ★ ★ THE DISGRACED ★ ★ ★ ★ ★ ★ ★ ★ ★ ★ ★

January–June 1863: Heads Turn West

After the Confederacy's resounding victory at Fredericksburg, Union hope sprang eternal in the West. Action in Tennessee had mixed results, but Grant's eight-month campaign in Vicksburg, Mississippi, and vicinity ended in victory.

☛ COLD DAYS AT STONES RIVER

As Lincoln regained his political footing after the defeat at Fredericksburg, Gen. William S. Rosecrans's Army of the Cumberland was in Nashville, 30 miles north of Braxton Bragg's Army of the Tennessee encampment at Murfreesboro. The Confederate goal was to protect the breadbasket of Tennessee and thwart Union movements toward Chattanooga.

Union general in chief Henry Halleck telegraphed Rosecrans and minced no words: "The Government demands action…if you cannot respond…someone else will be tried." So on December 26, 42,000 Union soldiers moved toward Murfreesboro.

The Union Line Holds Four days later Rosecrans's and Bragg's armies braved a bitterly cold, wet night as the generals planned the next day's encounter. Just after daybreak, as the Union soldiers were eating breakfast, 13,000 Johnny Rebs "swooped down on those Yankees," wrote a Tennessee soldier, "like a whirl-a-gust of woodpeckers in a hail storm."

In the fierce fighting that followed, the Confederates pushed the Union line back again and again, but it held—and grew stronger—with the arrival of reinforcements. On January 2, Bragg's men gained a brief advantage when they flushed a Union division from a bluff east of Stones River. The smaller Confederate force continued to hold their own but retreated on January 4. In the end, the desperate North claimed a Union victory.

☛ CHANCELLORSVILLE: Lee's "Perfect Battle"

In late April it was Joseph Hooker's turn to lead the Army of the Potomac across the Rappahannock River and try to reach Richmond. When word came that Robert E. Lee and his troops were on the march from Fredericksburg, Hooker halted his advance and gathered the Union corps at Chancellorsville.

Lee knew the only way he could defeat an army twice the size of his own was to divide his forces and strike where Union lines were most vulnerable. On May 1 he was told by Jeb Stuart that Hooker's right flank—Maj. Gen. Oliver O. Howard's 11th Corps—was exposed three miles west of Chancellorsville, so Lee and Stonewall Jackson planned a surprise attack.

Two Great Shocks Jackson's 30,000 soldiers took a circuitous course through deep woods and attacked early in the morning. Union soldiers fell by the thousands, and only when Hooker and Holmes hastily assembled a new line did Jackson's onslaught halt.

Entrenched Union soldiers fire on encroaching Rebels at Chancellorsville. Sheltering trenches were among the armies' most common fieldworks.

That night, Jackson and some of his officers rode into the darkness to reconnoiter. In a still-unexplained instance of friendly fire, shots rang out and Jackson was gravely wounded.

Over the next three days Lee outmaneuvered Hooker so expertly that the Union army's superior numbers meant nothing. What would later be called Lee's "perfect battle" was another shot in the arm for the South but a devastating blow to worried Northerners.

Stonewall's Fall Army surgeons determined that Stonewall Jackson's wounded left arm had to be amputated. The patient seemed all right until pneumonia set in. Informed on Sunday, May 10, that nothing could save him, Jackson reportedly said, "It is the Lord's day; my wish is fulfilled. I have always desired to die on Sunday."

The deeply religious general's wish was granted, and news of the hero's death shook the South to its roots. After lying in state at the capitol in Richmond, his body was taken to his Lexington, Virginia, home for burial.

☞ GRANT'S ROAD TO VICTORY AT VICKSBURG

By the fall of 1862, Ulysses S. Grant and William T. Sherman had become generals in the Army of the Tennessee—Grant as commander of the full army, Sherman as commander of a corps. Both realized ultimate victory would depend on Union control of the Mississippi River—and only the 250-mile stretch from Port Hudson, Louisiana, to Vicksburg, Mississippi, remained unoccupied. Taking Vicksburg was key, but the attempt would drag on for eight months.

Three Tries The first two attempts to attack hilly high-in-the-sky Vicksburg failed miserably.

★ In October, Grant and Sherman's bayou-and-land efforts to clear routes were for naught—not least

Lew Wallace: Officer Do-It-All

Lewis "Lew" Wallace was favored from the day of his birth in August 1827. His father, David, was a successful lawyer and politician, serving as a U.S. representative from Indiana and governor of the state; his mother, Zerelda Sanders Wallace, was a leader of the temperance and woman's suffrage movements. His great uncle was Revolutionary War naval hero John Paul Jones.

Like his father, Lew would practice law and enter politics, but he also served with distinction in the Civil War. He had a finger in the fields of literature, art, and design as well, as this timeline of accomplishments shows.

1856 • Elected to Indiana State Senate
   • Organized a Zouave militia, the Montgomery County Guards

1861 • Served as Adjutant General (chief administration officer) of Indiana at start of Civil War
   • Appointed colonel of 11th Indiana Volunteers

1862 • Promoted to major general and commanded divisions in battles of Fort Donelson and Shiloh
   • Fortified Cincinnati against General Bragg's foray into Kentucky and beyond

1864 • Credited with saving Washington, D.C. in the Battle of Monocacy (page 132)

1865 • Served as a military judge at the trial of Lincoln assassination conspirators
   • Sketched proceedings during the trial*
   • *The Fair God,* Wallace's first novel, is published

1878 • Served as governor of the New Mexico Territory

1880 • *Ben-Hur, A Tale of the Christ* is published**

1894 • Designed building for Ben-Hur Museum (now General Lew Wallace Study & Museum) in Crawfordsville, Indiana

* *An example is on display at the Smithsonian*
** *Became a worldwide best seller and remains in print. Silent film* Ben-Hur *(1925) starred Ramon Navarro; the 1959 remake, with Charleston Heston, broke box-office records and won 11 Oscars.*

because of cavalry raids by Nathan Bedford Forrest and Earl Van Dorn and skirmishes with soldiers led by Brig. Gen. John C. Pemberton, whose Army of Vicksburg guarded the city.

★ In winter, efforts to enlarge channels and dig canals seemed promising at first but collapsed, even with Rear Adm. David D. Porter exploring bayous and rivers. To make matters worse, Earl Van Dorn's cavalry destroyed the Union supply base at Holly Springs, Mississippi, in December.

> ... families found shelter in caves carved into hillsides. Thousands risked starvation as food grew scarcer and scarcer.

★ In May and June 1863 Grant's troops launched a series of attacks that led to brutal living conditions for Vicksburg citizens and Pemberton's army. As Union fire rained down and the delay of Confederate general Joseph E. Johnston's reinforcements stretched from days to weeks (the Union capture of the capital city of Jackson had thinned his troops), families found shelter in caves carved into the hillsides. Thousands risked starvation as food grew scarcer and scarcer.

The Siege's End The day after the Battle of Gettysburg, Pemberton surrendered the city of Vicksburg and his 30,000 soldiers. The date was July 4, 1863. With the surrender of Port Hudson on July 9, the Union had complete control of the Mississippi River, and the Confederacy had split in two.

Men in Charge, Part 3

Ambrose Burnside (pages 103, 131), the second commander of the Potomac Army, was succeeded by a New Englander and an American born overseas. Four other notable generals were among the 600,000-plus immigrants who joined the Union army.

☛ JOSEPH HOOKER (USA): "Fighting Joe"

The third commander of the Army of the Potomac was born and bred in Hadley, Massachusetts, and succeeded Ambrose Burnside in early 1863. Vain, handsome Joseph Hooker was called "Fighting Joe" because of his aggression in the field, and his military career was a roller coaster of successes and failures.

His highs came at Seven Days and Antietam, though at the latter a foot wound took him out of battle. He dipped low when he took a beating at Second Bull Run, and some of his wrong-headed decisions at Antietam are the stuff of legend.

Joe B. Gone Hooker's disputes with other brass were many. In June 1863 a heated argument at Army of the Potomac headquarters over force strength ended with Hooker's halfhearted "protest" resignation. President Lincoln and General Halleck jumped at the chance to replace the ornery general, and within days they had chosen George C. Meade as commander of the Army of the Potomac.

☛ GEORGE G. MEADE (USA): "Old Reliable"

Irish Catholic George Gordon Meade was born in the Spanish city of Cadiz because his father, a well-off Philadelphia merchant, served as a U.S. government naval agent there. Back in the States, Meade went to West Point, worked as a civil engineer, and began his career in the Union Army in August 1861 as commander of the Pennsylvania Reserves 2nd Brigade.

After joining the Army of the Potomac, he fought in Seven Days battles and suffered serious wounds. On his recovery, he became a division commander in the corps of Joseph Hooker, whom he would replace as commander of the Army of the Potomac in mid-1863. By then, he had come to be called "Old Reliable" for his skillfulness and steadiness.

George Gordon Meade

☛ FRANZ SIGEL (USA): Das Recruiter

Though Franz Sigel gained military experience in his native Germany, he went into public education after emigrating to America—first as a teacher in New York City, then as director of public schools in St. Louis. When war broke out, Sigel redonned a uniform as a colonel in the 3rd Missouri Infantry, and he would later be promoted to major general. His ability to recruit German immigrants to the Union Army made Sigel one of Lincoln's most effective political generals—and it earned him notoriety to boot. "I'm going to fight mit Sigel" morphed from a slogan into a popular song.

Pea Ridge Peak Militarily, Sigel excelled at the Battle of Pea Ridge but had little success thereafter. Still, he made his mark, as two imposing statues of Sigel on horseback attest—one in Forest Park in St. Louis, the other in Manhattan's Riverside Park.

☛ FREDERICK KNEFLER (USA): From Hungary to Indiana

A Jewish Hungarian, Frederick Knefler was the son of a respected physician. In 1850 he fled with his family to America in the wake of the Hungarian Revolution, and the Kneflers settled in Indianapolis.

Knefler's military career began in the 11th Indiana Infantry headed by Lew Wallace (page 112). The infantry successfully did its part at the Battle of Fort Donelson in Tennessee, and Knefler soon became Wallace's aide.

Patrick Cleburne, Hotshot

He was born in County Cork, Ireland, in 1828, orphaned at age 16, emigrated to the United States five years later, and settled in Helena, Arkansas. Arkansans welcomed Patrick Ronayne Cleburne, and the young Irishman became a successful businessman and community leader.

In January 1861 he joined the 15th Arkansas Company C (the Yell Rifles), and by December 1862 had been promoted to major general in the Army of Tennessee. Valor and well-honed military skills were Cleburne's hallmarks as he fought his way through the battles of Stones River, Chickamauga, and Atlanta.

Cleburne stirred controversy in early 1864, when he proposed that slaves be enlisted to fill the depleted Confederate ranks and, in turn, win their freedom. His idea that slavery was the Confederacy's "most vulnerable point, a continued embarrassment, and in some respects an insidious weakness" won him no points with higher-ups from Jefferson Davis on down, and the proposal was dead on arrival.

The 35-year-old Cleburne met his own end later that year at the Battle of Franklin, and he lies buried in his adopted city of Helena. A monument to the valiant soldier was dedicated in Franklin, Tennessee, in 2006.

★ ★ ★ ★ ★ ★ ★ ★ ★ ★ ★ ★   THE CELEBRATED   ★ ★ ★ ★ ★ ★ ★ ★ ★ ★ ★ ★

In August 1862 Knefler was made commanding colonel of the 79th Indiana Infantry and saw action in the battles of Stones River, Chickamauga, and Missionary Ridge, where he led a daring charge up the ridge. After a second successful charge at the Battle of Nashville, he was awarded the rank of brigadier general.

Back home after the war, Knefler opened a successful law practice, headed the Indianapolis pension office, and became a noted civic leader. In 1899, as president of the Soldiers and Sailors Monument board of regents, he laid the cornerstone of the downtown Indianapolis landmark.

The Rank and File

It is estimated that some 2.1 million soldiers served in the Union Army over the course of the war and 900,000 in the Confederate Army. Those bound for combat rather than special-unit assignments, such as ambulance corps and signalmen, put their lives on the line for a cause—and roughly one out of five would die for it.

———◦((◦))◦———

July–December 1863: Gettysburg to Chattanooga

Jefferson Davis and General Lee agreed that a northern victory was the next step for the Army of Northern Virginia, not only to daunt the North but to help weaken General Grant's grip on Vicksburg. But stumbles were in store for the Confederacy.

☞ FIRESTORM AT GETTYSBURG

The war's most famous battle started inadvertently. Confederate Lt. Gen. A. P. Hill led a division to Gettysburg after reports that badly needed shoes were warehoused there. Union major general John Buford lay in wait, and on the morning of July 1, Buford's mounted soldiers surprised Hill's troops as they entered the town.

So began three days of assaults and retreats at Devil's Den, Little Round Top, Cemetery Hill, and other now-familiar swaths of hallowed ground as Rebel forces led by generals such as Robert E. Lee, James Longstreet, and Jubal Early went up against the larger armies of George C. Meade, Winfield Scott Hancock, and others.

Chamberlain's Call On the second day, Meade ordered the 20th Maine regiment of Brig. Gen. Joshua Chamberlain

How the Armies Were Organized

The Union and Confederate armies were divided in progressively larger units, starting with small **companies.** To varying degrees, the larger organizational levels of manpower were home to **infantry** (foot soldiers), **cavalry** (mounted soldiers), and **artillery** (soldiers armed with large-caliber weapons or cannons).

★ **Companies** The basic units, usually of about 100 men

★ **Regiments** Made up of 100 or so companies and usually designated by state and number (e.g., 34th Indiana)

★ **Brigades** Generally comprised of three to six regiments, but in the South as many as fifteen

★ **Divisions** Large bodies of soldiers generally composed of three or four brigades in the North and four to six in the South.

★ **Corps** Made up of divisions—two or three in the North, and as many as four in the South. Roman numerals were generally used to designate corps (e.g., XI for 11th—or Eleventh—Corps).

★ **Armies** Comprised of corps of varying number—usually from one up to eight or nine. An exception was the Union's Army of the Potomac, which over the course of the war has 25 corps, two being cavalry corps.

(page 105), to defend Little Round Top "at all costs." After four hours of bloody assaults, hundreds of Chamberlain's men were wounded and the 20th Maine had run out of ammunition.

When Chamberlain spied the enemy assembling for a final attack, he was forced to improvise. He shouted an order to "Fix bayonets!" and charge. Racing down Little Round Top's slopes, the 20th Maine caught the enemy off guard. The stunned Rebels had to run or be taken prisoner. The Union line stayed intact, setting the stage for Lee's full-frontal assault on July 3.

Lee's Angst Against James Longstreet's advice, Lee sent 13,000 men into an open field to face Union artillery. Fully half would be killed or wounded. The North won a profound victory, and as Lee retreated, he cried to his men, "It is all my fault." George Meade could have said the same of himself when he failed to pursue Lee's 14-mile-long line of forces and let a chance to end the war slip away.

Lincoln's 278 Words

President Lincoln spoke immortal words on November 19, 1863, at the dedication of the Soldiers National Cemetery at Gettysburg. The man who preceded him, famed orator Edward Everett, gave a speech that ran to 13,500 words and lasted for two hours. Lincoln's Gettysburg Address totaled 278 words—and not because he dashed if off on his way to the ceremony, as myth has it. Lincoln wrote and rewrote what is considered one of history's most eloquent and moving orations well in advance.

☛ BLACKS JOIN THE RANKS

Black militias had been mustered even before the Emancipation Proclamation became official on January 1, 1863. The 1st Louisiana Native Guards, for one, had fought fearlessly when the Union captured Port Hudson in the wake of the fall of Vicksburg, putting the lie to the notion that blacks would not measure up as soldiers.

The Massachusetts 54th The most famous black regiment was the 54th Massachusetts Volunteer Infantry, recruited by white abolitionists and led by Col. Robert Gould Shaw, a Boston Brahmin (all commanders in black units were white).

On July 18 the 54th led an attack on Fort Wagner as part of the Union campaign to capture Charleston Harbor. The

Confederates were so dug in on three sides that a Union defeat was almost a foregone conclusion.

The valor of the 54th was trumpeted by the press as the win. "In the midst of shot and shell," wrote one correspondent, "they pushed their way, reached the fort, gained the parapet, and for nearly half an hour held their ground and did not fall until nearly every commissioned officer was shot down." One man shot down was Colonel Shaw, whose body the Rebels threw into a mass grave with his soldiers—a burial place his abolitionist family considered honorable.

Unequal Footing Redressed That blacks were paid less and had fewer benefits than white soldiers was a matter of grave concern. In August, Frederick Douglass met with President Lincoln in the White House and put forth his case for equal pay, equal protection, and the right to promotion. Lincoln listened.

Congress was slow to act—but in March 1865 (a month before Lee's surrender) legislators passed the Enrollment Act, which granted retroactive equal pay to black soldiers.

From May 1863, United States Colored Troops (USCT) were recruited from all states. Shown here is the 107th Colored Infantry Provost Guard.

The Draft Riots of 1863

In New York City a rigorous version of the draft law passed after the Emancipation Proclamation brought simmering ethnic tensions to a boil; as of March 1863, all white men between the ages of 20 and 35 could be drafted, but blacks (considered non-citizens) could not. Moreover, white proslavery Democrats—Irish immigrants, in particular—feared losing jobs to blacks.

On the morning of July 13, what started as attacks on buildings became assaults on black men, some unspeakable in their viciousness. In late afternoon, a huge mob crashed into the Colored Orphans Asylum on Fifth Avenue, looted it as staff escorted children to safety, and burned it down.

By the time the riot ended on July 17, scores of people were dead and working-class whites had announced loud and clear that New York had no room for blacks—though some upper-crust whites, Republican newspaper offices, and Protestant churches had been targeted as well.

A Welcome Alliance On the other side of the coin, the elite Union League Club made a statement of its own. In December, Secretary of War Edwin M. Stanton permitted the club to raise a black regiment. Club members were aided by the Garrison Literary and Benevolent Society, formed years before by Henry Highland Garnet (page 30) and other radical black abolitionists.

☞ SPIES AT WORK

Espionage was often part and parcel of Civil War strategies. Allen B. Pinkerton served as George B. McClellan's intelligence chief until Little Mac left the Army of the Potomac. Pinkerton's successor, George H. Sharpe, a New York lawyer-turned-colonel, helped found the Bureau of Military Information and developed intelligence methods still in use. The Confederacy plowed great sums of money into secret service activities, and their Signal Service sent couriers back and forth to the North until the war's end.

Three Civilian Agents Nonmilitary men and women also got into the act, too:

★ Henry Harrison, a failed actor from Tennessee, became a full-time Rebel spy and whispered to James Longstreet that Union troops were massing at Gettysburg.

★ Washington gentlewoman Rose O'Neil Greenhow directed a band of Confederate intelligence gatherers and tipped General Beauregard off that Union general McDowell was advancing on Bull Run.

★ Intelligence on Rebel positions on South Carolina's Combahee River—provided by Harriet Tubman, who did some spying on the side—enabled Union colonel James Montgomery to raid plantations, destroy bridges, and free 750 slaves.

☛ A CONTRABAND CONCERT FOR MR. LINCOLN

Aunt Mary Dines was a slave who escaped to Washington, D.C., and became a beloved teacher at the Duff Green's Row contraband camp on Capitol Hill. In *They Knew Lincoln* (1942), author John E. Washington retold her story of the day President Lincoln went to hear the fugitives sing, in 1863:

> *All of the people dressed in their best clothes...*
> *Some men and boys had on soldiers' cast-off blue*
> *uniforms and some had on old rebel uniforms they*
> *had picked up after the rebels had been driven away*
> *by the Yankees.*
>   *Presently President Lincoln and his wife...got*
> *out of their carriages. Uncle Ben, the oldest slave*
> *in the camp, was called on [to pray], and he called*
> *upon every saint in the Bible to bless President*
> *Lincoln and his good lady. When he was through,*

all stood up and sang "My Country 'Tis of Thee" and
President Lincoln took off his hat and sang, too.

Aunt Mary said she never forgot how her knees
shook as she opened the [program] with "Nobody
Knows the Trouble I See, But Jesus"...To her great
surprise, she saw President Lincoln wiping the tears
off his face with his bare hands.

☛ THE MOVE TO CHATTANOOGA

As the world focused on Gettysburg, Union general William S. Rosecrans's Army of the Cumberland was successfully pushing the Rebels out of central Tennessee and toward the vital transportation hub of Chattanooga. On August 16, 60,000 Union troops began a week-long advance culminating in the occupation of the city as Braxton Bragg's surprised and outnumbered forces retreated.

Interruption at Chickamauga Bragg's forces had retreated to the north Georgia mountains with Rosecrans in pursuit. On September 19 a chance meeting of enemy patrols at Chickamauga Creek led to the West's deadliest battle. When, on the second day, a confused Rosecrans inadvertently opened a huge gap in his defensive line, James Longstreet's fighters surged through and wreaked havoc on Union forces.

Rosecrans left the field as George Henry Thomas (page 105) pulled the troops back together in one of the most courageous stands of the war.

Taking the Prize Surrounded by Rebels, Chattanooga remained in Union hands—and Lincoln and Grant knew how vital the region was to a Union victory. Grant replaced Rosecrans with Thomas and sent major reinforcements to the scene.

When the Battle of Chattanooga erupted in late November, the Union captured Orchard Knob, Lookout Mountain, and seemingly impregnable Missionary Ridge. The "Gateway to the Lower

Pity the Poor Prisoner

Neither the North or the South was prepared to manage a flood of captured soldiers. During the war more than 400,000 prisoners were housed in 150 facilities, and around an eighth of them died from exposure to the elements, unsanitary conditions, toxic water or food, or a lack of medical care.

The Hellhole in Georgia The worst prison was Camp Sumter, located in southern Georgia and better known as Andersonville, after the nearby hamlet. An estimated 45,000 Union prisoners were crammed into the hellish 26-acre stockade in its 14 months of existence. Describing the camp's one stream, a prisoner wrote: "The water is perfectly reeking with offal and poison. Still men drink it and die."

Issuing rations at Andersonville Prison

Andersonville's commandant was Capt. Henry Wirz, who after the war became the first American tried for war crimes. He was hanged, yet claimed his innocence to the end. "I know what orders are," he said, "and I am being hung for obeying them." He may have been right: John H. Winder, the Confederate officer who oversaw prison camps in Georgia and Alabama, had died the previous February—and Wirz was the one left to blame.

Andersonville Postmortem After the war, Clara Barton—founder of the Red Cross—worked to locate missing soldiers. She met a former inmate who had kept a list of the soldiers buried in graves marked only by numbered sticks, so the dead were ID'd and the graves properly marked.

Today the Andersonville National Historic Site is also home to the Prisoner of War Museum, with exhibits on prisoner-of-war camps throughout history.

South" was theirs, and Chattanooga would be Sherman's supply and logistics base for his march through Atlanta and on to the sea.

Uncommon Warriors

Each of the three million people—men and women—who fought in the war had a story. However, very few personal histories came to the surface and lived on. Here, briefly, are six.

☞ BENJAMIN W. OWENS (CSA): 12 Days to Glory

Young Benjamin Welch Owens, born and raised in West River, Maryland, enlisted in the 1st Maryland Artillery on June 3, 1863. The artillery was part of Confederate general Richard S. Ewell's Second Corps, which was called by Robert E. Lee to head to Pennsylvania in what came to be called the Gettysburg Campaign.

Owen's Brave Act On June 13 the corps reached Winchester, Virginia, where a Union garrison blocked their path. In the third and final day of the Battle of Second Winchester, Private Owens was one of the few in his unit who escaped death or wounding at the Stephenson's Depot railroad bridge. He single-handedly held off Union forces with repeated cannon fire until reinforcements arrived, and the Rebels took the garrison.

Eight decades later, in 1993, Owens was posthumously awarded the Confederate Medal of Honor—the only Marylander so honored.

☞ PVT. VALENTINE C. RANDOLPH (USA): Diarist

Numerous soldiers on both sides kept diaries, but few privates were better educated than Valentine C. Randolph, who brought his Latin and Greek textbooks along when he joined

39th Illinois regiment. These two excerpts contrast a calm day with a combative one.

An entry from 1861, as the 39th Illinois reached Indiana on its train journey from St. Louis to Virginia:

> *Oct. 30: The Hoosiers along our route seemed very patriotic but none more so than a lass who threw kisses with both hands at the soldiers as the cars passed by. The citizens of Indianapolis prepared breakfast for us…Some [soldiers], by acting the hog, which animal they more resemble in their manners than a man, got as much as they wanted to eat and waste, others got but little.*

And one from 1863, when Randolph's regiment was among the land forces deployed in a failed Union attempt to take Charleston Harbor:

> *July 20: Under a tropical sun we lay in the ditch, the sand was scorching hot. If a man stood up straight he was liable to get a Rebel bullet in his head. A little after noon the regiment fell back, excepting 100 men who were left in the pits to act as sharpshooters.*

☛ ROBERT SMALLS (USA): From Fugitive to Captain

As a slave, Robert Smalls was referred to as a wheelman, not captain, on the USS *Planter,* the Confederate transport ship he piloted in Charleston Harbor. But his knowledge of the codes and signals that would get him past checkpoints and to the Union fleet blockading the harbor was as worthy as any naval superior's.

In the wee hours of May 13, 1862, Smalls, his family, and several black crewmen boarded the *Planter.* Smalls safely passed five forts and soon reached a welcoming Union ship.

Free and Famous After turning the *Planter* over as contraband and offering intelligence to the Union Navy, Smalls became something of a celebrity. He even met briefly with President Lincoln.

After the war, Smalls entered politics in his native South Carolina. The man who had taken his destiny into his own hands served two terms in the South Carolina legislature and three in the U.S. House of Representatives.

☛ O. S. PHILIP BAZAAR (USA): Bravery at Fort Fisher

When Ordinary Seaman Philip Bazaar, a Chilean immigrant, joined the Union Navy, he was assigned to Adm. David D. Porter's USS *Santiago de Cuba*. And a Medal of Honor was probably the last thing on this personable swab's mind.

Bringing Down "Gibraltar" After David Farragut captured Mobile Bay in August 1864, the only Confederate seaport open to trade was Wilmington, North Carolina, guarded by heavily fortified Fort Fisher—a.k.a. the "Gibraltar of the South." In early December, 1864, General Grant sent land and sea forces to topple the fort, and a 12-week siege began.

During the final (and successful) assault, Bazaar was one of six crew members who braved heavy fire to enter Fort Fisher and deliver dispatches from Porter to army commander Alfred Terry. The feat won Bazaar and his mates the Medal of Honor.

Medals of Honor Naval Medals of Honor came into being in December 1861 and were awarded to petty officers, seamen, and Marines who "most distinguished themselves by their gallantry during the present war." The Union Army followed suit and began issuing medals in the summer of 1862.

Union Navy Medal of Honor

☛ LORETA ELENA VELÁZQUEZ (CSA): Soldier, Spy

Loreta Velázquez was a mystery. She was born to a well-off Cuban family in 1842, studied in New Orleans, and married a Texas army officer before she turned 16.

As the war broke out and her husband donned a Confederate uniform, Velázquez begged to accompany him to the front. When he would have no part of it, she had a tailor whip up a uniform anyway. She also adopted the unlikely name of Harry T. Buford.

Velázquez's Great Adventure Her husband was killed soon afterward, and Velázquez embarked on a four-year career alternately fighting battles as a man (First Bull Run, Shiloh) and spying for the Confederacy as a woman. She later told her story, some of which was received with skepticism, in *The Woman in Battle: A Narrative of the Exploits, Adventures, and Travels of Madame Loreta Janeta Veláquez, Otherwise Known as Lieutenant Harry T. Buford, Confederate States Army* (1876).

☛ SARAH ROSETTA WAKEMAN: A Secret Kept

Young Sarah Wakeman didn't like doing chores around her parents' farm in Afton, New York—especially since they paid nothing. So she dressed as a man and took a job shoveling coal on a canal boat.

Sarah's Short-Lived Scam Upriver, Wakeman met soldiers from 153rd New York State Volunteers and liked the sound of what they earned. So in August 1862 she enlisted in the regiment as Lyons Wakefield. The military life took her to Washington, D.C., and then to Louisiana, where she fell victim to one of the Civil War soldier's common plagues: dysentery.

She died in a New Orleans military hospital in June 1864. And she had fooled everyone with whom she served. A tombstone engraved "Pvt. Lyons Wakefield" marks her grave at Chalmette National Cemetery in St. Bernard Parish.

January 1864–April 1865:
The Road to Appomattox

In March 1864 Lincoln promoted Grant to general in chief of all Union armies and put Sherman in his place as commander of Western Theater armies. Together the men whose bond was forged at Shiloh would now wage total war by confiscating or destroying southerners' property and sapping their will to resist.

☛ DEATH IN THE WILDERNESS

General in chief Grant literally stayed in the saddle as the Army of the Potomac moved toward Richmond at the start of the Overland Campaign, joining his soldiers in the field. As his troops slowed to a crawl in the dark, densely forested area of northeast Virginia known as the Wilderness, General Lee's army attacked. Confusion and chaos reigned as 70,000 Union soldiers fought nearly 40,000 Rebels.

Retreat wasn't an option for Grant, and he advanced the troops 12 miles south to Spotsylvania Courthouse—a morale booster for his battered men.

> The fighting that preceded and followed this 18-hour battle, much of it hand-to hand, was the most savage of the war.

The Battle of Spotsylvania On May 12, 15,000 screaming Yankees descended on Rebels dug into a complex web of trenches. They split Lee's army and captured most of the soldiers of the celebrated Stonewall division. The fighting that preceded and followed this 18-hour battle, much of it hand-to-hand, was the most savage of the war. There was no clear-cut winner at Spotsylvania, but the cost of more than 10 days of combat was staggering: 18,000 casualties for Grant, 12,000 for Lee.

Halleck Out, Grant In

Henry Wager Halleck, born in 1815 in the shadow of New York's Adirondack Mountains, made Phi Beta Kappa at Union College and graduated third in his class of 64 at West Point, where cadets christened him "Old Brains." It was there, as a faculty member in the early 1840s, that he first laid eyes on Ulysses S. Grant.

When Halleck was commander of the Department of the Missouri (page 85), he doubted the brigadier general's ability to pull off the capture of Forts Henry and Donelson. The reason? Grant's reputation for drinking. Yet two years to the month later, Grant would replace Halleck as general in chief of the Union Army.

Grant and the Bottle Historians differ on how fond Grant was for alcohol but believe he always chose duty over the bottle. He went on the occasional bender, and boredom could drive him to tippling—but whiskey never got the best of him. In fact, it's said that President Lincoln told an officer who griped about Grant's habit, "Find out what he drinks and send a barrel of it to my other generals!"

☛ SOUTH TO COLD HARBOR

On May 31 Union general Phillip Sheridan seized the junction at the crossroads of Cold Harbor and struggled to hold it against entrenched Rebel forces. Grant and Lee beefed up their armies to 109,000 and 59,000, and more rivers of blood were about to flow.

On the third day of battle, Grant ordered a full-front assault on the Rebel trenches. His soldiers were hit with a blaze of gunfire, and 7,000 bluecoats fell in short order. A year after Lee unwittingly ordered his men on a suicide mission at Gettysburg, Grant did the same at Cold Harbor.

Collateral Damage As casualties mounted, so did war resistance in the North. Peace Democrats, who had pushed for negotiation over combat, began to call Grant a "butcher." And the prospect of another four years for President Lincoln looked less likely by the month.

☛ THE SIEGE OF PETERSBURG BEGINS

In the days after the debacle at Cold Harbor, Grant decided to move south of Richmond and capture the Confederate supply-and-transportation hub of Petersburg. His forces succeeded in cutting a railroad from Petersburg to northeast North Carolina, but only after a month-long battle. By then Lee's army had arrived to reinforce Petersburg's defenses, and both sides settled in for a battle of wits and arms that would last for eight long months.

Battle of the Crater The siege started with a bang on July 30. A key Rebel fortification was close to the Union line held by Gen. Ambrose Burnside, and an officer whose regiment was full of Pennsylvania coal miners suggested they tunnel under Confederate lines, lay a charge, and then blow the fort up. Grant and Meade were skeptical, but the miners managed to dig a 511-foot tunnel in just over a month. When the gunpowder (four tons) was in place, Burnside was to explode it and then lead troops through the gap and attack.

The Blow-Up Backfires The explosion blew a huge crater into the earth and knocked out a Rebel regiment. But Burnside lost control of his troops, many of whom descended into the 30-foot-deep crater instead of pursuing the

Grant rarely wore his full uniform, but here he was camera-ready.

enemy. Soldiers aboveground also fell out of line, and the Rebels gained the upper hand. The result was 6,000 casualties, more than half of them Yankees. Another casualty was Burnside's career, and the Union Army received a giant black eye.

☛ ATTACK ON WASHINGTON FOILED!

Jubal Early couldn't have been the only Confederate general who wanted to raid Washington, D.C., and, at the very least, score a moral victory. But he came the closest.

On July 9, after marching north from the Shenandoah Valley and gathering reinforcements along the way, Early found Union general Lew Wallace's division blocking the bridge over the Monocacy River. A 10-hour battle ensued, and the Rebels fought off the Union soldiers and crossed the bridge.

The Battle of Monocacy A day later Early's army stood six miles from Washington, D.C., with the Capitol dome in sight. Washingtonians knew it, and worried that the raw recruits manning the city's fortifications wouldn't be able to protect them.

General Grant, in the meantime, had time to dispatch extra troops from Petersburg, thanks to the one-day delay. Early's forces were turned back. If it were not for the Battle of Monocacy—known as the "battle that saved Washington" (and no small skirmish, considering the 1,300 killed), the feisty general might have achieved his goal.

☛ SHERMAN TARGETS ATLANTA

On May 4 William T. Sherman left Chattanooga with 100,000 soldiers from the Army of the Cumberland, Army of the Tennessee, and Army of the Ohio. The destination was Atlanta, the Confederate transportation hub a hundred miles south.

From July 20th to the 28th, battles at Peachtree Creek, Atlanta, and Ezra Church were fought on the edge of the city.

When he evacuated Atlanta, General Hood tried to burn anything useful to the Yankees, including his ordinance train and the Schofield Rolling Mill.

The Confederates, led by the hard-fighting John Bell Hood (who had just replaced cautious Joe Johnston), would keep the Union forces at bay, at the cost of 15,000 of Hood's 50,000-man army. But the Union noose tightened as Yankees encircled the city and destroyed supply lines while fending off bands of Rebels.

A Clever Distraction In late August the wily Sherman moved south to Jonesboro—the site of Hood's last supply line, the Montgomery and Atlanta Railroad—and left the impression he had withdrawn from the fight. Atlantans celebrated in the streets, and the South breathed a sigh of relief.

However, on August 30 Sherman surprised one and all by destroying the railroad at Jonesboro. Two days later a shaken Hood evacuated Atlanta and burned any installations useful to the enemy. In doing so, he ignited the famous Burning of Atlanta. In ashes or whole, the city was in Union hands once and for all.

☛ FARRAGUT TAKES MOBILE BAY

On the maritime front, only one strategically important port in the Gulf of Mexico remained in Confederate hands and open to trade from abroad: Mobile Bay, guarded by Fort Gaines and Fort Morgan. On August 5 Adm. David Farragut led 14 wooden ships and four ironclads into the bay channel and incurred a hail of fire from the forts. It took Farragut's navy three weeks to prevail—and though the upriver city of Mobile wasn't captured, the port was sealed off.

Torpedoes Be Damned The battle is best remembered for a moment that seems straight out of a movie. Mobile Bay was lined with mines (then called torpedoes), and one sank a Union ironclad. But instead of retreating, an inspired Union fleet fought on after Farragut—who had lashed to himself the flagship's masthead—cried out, "Damn the torpedoes! Full speed ahead!"

They Also "Served"

More than a few famous names took part in the war, some more seriously than others. For these two men, soldiering was but a blip in a fabled career.

★ **Mark Twain** In May 1861 the young man whose real name was Samuel Clemens impulsively joined a Rebel militia in the border state of Missouri. Clemens, who later said, "We left which side we were on to the God of Battles," recounted his 1861 stint as a soldier in the story "A Private History of a Campaign That Failed."

★ **Jesse James** Future outlaw Jesse James joined the guerilla army led by William "Bloody Bill" Anderson and was one of 80 guerillas who took part in the September 1864 Battle of Centralia, Missouri—remembered less for the combat than for Anderson's contemptible capture and execution of 23 unarmed Union soldiers.

Poetry and War

In the early 1860s the abolitionist Thomas Wentworth Higginson (page 31) wrote about slave uprisings for the *Atlantic Monthly* and, off topic, published a "Letter to a Young Contributor," which advised young writers on how get published. Soon, four poems arrived in the mail from a 32-year-old Amherst woman named Emily Dickinson. Higginson became Dickinson's editor, and two decades of friendship followed.

Higginson's Colored Regiment Higginson's literary sensibilities didn't keep him from fighting in the Civil War. In fact, he commanded a regiment of freed slaves—the 1st South Carolina Volunteers—and traveled the South recruiting black men for the Union Army. At his funeral on May 13, 1911, the casket was wrapped in the 1st South Carolina Volunteers flag. Earlier he had told his story—and theirs—in *Army Life in a Black Regiment* (1869).

☛ LINCOLN KEEPS HIS JOB

From the start of 1864, so-called Radical Republicans (immediate abolitionists who loathed the South) had fished about for a candidate to replace Lincoln in the November election. And they weren't the only war-weary Americans who believed the president couldn't be reelected in the fall—Lincoln himself doubted he would be voted back in.

Broadening the Base Things changed in June, when Republicans formed the temporary National Union Party. This name was used to attract War Democrats who would never vote Republican. The party nominated Lincoln, but his Radical Republican–leaning vice president Hannibal Hamlin was replaced with pro-war Democrat Andrew Johnson. General Sherman's early September capture of Atlanta would also brighten Lincoln's prospects.

In November, Lincoln was reelected—and overwhelmingly. His Democratic opponent was George B. McClellan, the former general in whom Lincoln had once placed great faith.

☛ THE ALMOST-FINAL PUSH

In the last few months of 1864, total-war tactics would pay off for the Union and devastate parts of Virginia and Georgia.

Sheridan's Shenandoah Campaign Beginning in August, Union general Philip Sheridan laid waste to the Virginia valley, called the "breadbasket of the Confederacy" (page 107)— and in the process took down the Shenandoah's biggest Rebel troublemaker, Jubal Early. In mid-October, when Sheridan was on his way to Washington, Early silently moved four divisions into position and at dawn attacked Sheridan's army near Cedar Creek, capturing 1,300 prisoners and 18 guns.

Sheridan rushed back and, in the war's greatest example of battlefield leadership, roused his men and drove Early's forces across the creek to recapture the guns and 23 more. What was left of Early's army joined Lee at Petersburg.

Sherman's March In mid-November, William T. Sherman and 62,000 soldiers in two columns began a 300-mile march to sea that would leave a large swath of death and destruction behind. Union soldiers fought off weakened Rebel troops as they moved through Milledgeville (then the Georgia state capital), Honey Hill, and beyond.

On December 21 Sherman reached the picture-perfect city of Savannah and sent Lincoln what is perhaps the war's most famous telegram: "I beg to present you as a Christmas gift, the city of Savannah, with one hundred and fifty heavy guns and plenty of ammunition and also about twenty-five thousand bales of cotton."

☛ THE THRASHING IN NASHVILLE

As Tennessee's capital city readied for Christmas, the war's most brilliant tactical battle destroyed John Bell Hood's

Gen. John B. Hood

Confederate Army of Tennessee. On the morning of December 15, Union general George H. Thomas attacked Hood's right flank alongside Hillsboro Pike and kept it contained all day as Union forces pummeled the Rebel left.

When fighting died down that night, Hood's army retreated two miles south to Overton Hill, only to face a Union repeat performance the next day. Hood's army collapsed, and the thousands unable to escape surrendered.

Hood Gives In for Good The much-feared Nathan Bedford Forrest commanded the Rebel rear guard, which kept the pursuing Union cavalry at bay as the escapees made their way to Alabama and into Mississippi. On January 13 the tattered remains of the Confederate Army of Tennessee reached Tupelo, where an exhausted and broken Hood resigned his command.

Fletcher Harper, War Archivist

In the early 1800s four brothers named Harper would move from a farm in New York's Hudson Valley to the peak of publishing in Manhattan. Printers James and John began publishing books as J. & J. Harper in 1817. Younger brothers Fletcher and Joseph joined them a few years later, and Harper & Brothers (Later Harper & Row and now HarperCollins) was off and running.

Fletcher Harper is credited with the 1850 founding of the journal *Harper's Weekly*. From the start of the Civil War to the end, the journal had no peer in updating Americans on the war and the officers and soldiers who fought it. Descriptions of battles rarely left a stone unturned, and detailed illustrations bought the reality of warfare home. Twenty-first century readers can see for themselves by accessing facsimile copies of Civil War–era *Harper's Weekly* online.

★ ★ ★ ★ ★ ★ ★ ★ ★ ★ ★ [CHRONICLERS] ★ ★ ★ ★ ★ ★ ★ ★ ★ ★ ★

☞ THE END

The Confederacy's last gasp began on March 2 when Philip Sheridan finished off the last shreds of Jubal Early's army at Waynesboro; grew softer with a failed attack on Grant's center at Fort Steadman, on Petersburg's outskirts; and then died down to a whisper on April 1 as the Union Army broke Lee's Petersburg lines. As Lee's forces evacuated and headed toward Appomattox, the War Department told Jefferson Davis, "General Lee telegraphs he can hold his position no longer."

Richmond Reclaimed Davis and the army quickly left Richmond, but not before ordering that arsenals and factories be burned. Union soldiers brought the fires and looters under control, and when President Lincoln and his son Tad toured the vanquished city on April 3, American flags fluttered above.

☞ LEE'S SURRENDER

On April 6 Robert E. Lee's army clashed with Union troops near the Appomattox River. Early the next morning a Confederate

Terms of surrender were agreed upon in the parlor of a private residence.

rider carrying a white flag told Union officers that General Lee wished to meet with General Grant. Lee arrived first in the tiny town of Appomattox Court House. He knew the southern cause was lost and was prepared to surrender his army. But what would Grant want? Revenge or reconciliation?

Dignity on Both Sides Thanks to the wisdom of two like-minded generals, the terms of surrender were simple, humane, and honorable. Grant pledged that if Lee's men laid down their weapons and went home, there would be no reprisals. Knowing that most of the Johnny Rebs would be returning to long-neglected farms, Grant let them keep their horses and mules. As news of Lee's surrender spread among the Union troops, they started firing artillery in celebration, until Grant ordered the cannons silenced. Peace had begun.

The Last to Die

Skirmishes along the way brought Union reinforcements, including the 34th Indiana Infantry. The Rebel cavalry sprang into action, and on May 13, 1865, the Battle of Palmito Ranch became the last land battle of the Civil War. The Confederates prevailed in their last hurrah, with 30 casualties to the Union's 111.

R.I.P. John J. Williams Records show that the last soldier to die in America's most costly war was Indianan John Jefferson Williams. The 22 year old had joined Company B of the 34th Indiana in September 1863, but Palmito Ranch was the first—and last—battle he fought.

Williams's grave can be found at Alexandria National Cemetery at Pineville, Louisiana. The life he lived can be glimpsed at the outstanding war veterans museum in his hometown—the Museum of the Soldier, in Portland, Indiana.

THE CAREGIVERS

During the Civil War, men and women from all walks of life either enlisted or volunteered to care for the diseased, wounded, and dying. It was no small task: More American soldiers were treated in Civil War hospitals—from tents at the edge of a battlefield to nearby homes or barns—than in the two world wars combined.

———— ((◉)) ————

Advancements in the Field

Necessity was often the mother of invention as the bloody war wore on, and battlefield medicine spurred progress in fields such as sanitation, ambulatory care, embalming, and nursing.

☛ WOMEN TO THE RESCUE

While surgical procedures were in the hands of male doctors, nursing and other hospital duties were almost entirely the province of women.

In the North By the summer of 1861, thousands of local relief groups had sprung in northern states. The most prominent was the Woman's Central Relief Association in New York, one of whose founders was Elizabeth Blackwell, the first female doctor in the United States. In June the groups were coordinated with the establishment of the U.S. Sanitary Commission.

Longtime charity workers Jane Hoge and Mary Livermore of Chicago furthered the commission's goal to inspect and improve sanitary conditions at camps and hospitals and provide nursing care and medical supplies.

In the South One of the most active of the hundreds of organizations was the Women's Relief Society of the Confederate

This crowded Union field hospital was located at Savage's Station, Virginia, the site of one of the Seven Days battles (page 94).

States, presided over by Felicia Grundy Porter of Nashville, Tennessee. Porter set up local hospitals and raised money for artificial limbs by arranging benefit concerts in cities and towns across the state. A prime example of the many state-sponsored organizations across the Confederacy was the Georgia Relief and Hospital Association.

☛ JONATHAN LETTERMAN: "Father of Battlefield Medicine"

As soon as Pennsylvania-born Dr. Jonathan Letterman graduated from medical school (1849), he joined the Army Medical Department as an assistant surgeon. Assigned to the Army of the Potomac at the start of the Civil War, he became the army's medical director in mid-1862.

Even in this second year of the war, surgeons and nurses worked against a background of chaos. In battles with thousands of casualties, many of the wounded had to fend for themselves for hours, if not days.

Important Firsts Letterman brought order to mayhem with a barrage of innovations:

- ★ First ambulance corps
- ★ First triage system
- ★ First three-stage evacuation system
  (dressing station, field hospital, regular hospital)

In 1866 Letterman published *Medical Recollections of the Army of the Potomac*. After the death of his wife in 1872, he was plagued with depression and illness. He died at age 48 that same year and lies buried at Arlington National Cemetery.

☞ SAMUEL P. MOORE: Southern Surgeon General

Samuel Preston Moore, the son of a Charleston banker, graduated from the Medical College of South Carolina and opened a medical practice in Little Rock, Arkansas, in 1835. The next year, he joined the U.S. Army as an assistant surgeon. By the Civil War, Moore's reputation was such that Jefferson Davis appointed him Surgeon General of the Confederate Army.

Meeting the Challenge Over the course of the war, Dr. Moore took the number of experienced army surgeons from 24 to 3,000-plus, all of whom had to pass muster at Moore's new medical boards; developed 32-bed huts that fit together to form modular field hospitals; and set up laboratories to process traditional herbal medicines as a substitute for blockaded medicines.

Moore's Manual In 1864 Moore published a training manual for surgeons, titled *Confederate States Medical and Journal*, complete with descriptions and drawings of medical procedures. Though methodical, its notations brought a touch of humanity to the injury or death of legions of sons, brothers, and fathers. An example:

Case 7.—J. A., a private of company "B" 38th Virginia infantry, was admitted July 3rd, 1862, with compound comminuted [pulverized] fracture of upper-third of thigh bone…Patient died of exhaustion [bodily collapse] July 6th.

The Art of Embalming

The first officer to die in the Civil War—on May 24, 1861—was also one of its most promising: 24-year-old colonel Elmer Ellsworth, who gained fame when he ripped down a Confederate flag flying at an Alexandria, Virginia, inn and was shot dead by the innkeeper. Ellsworth had become close friends with Abraham and Mary Lincoln when he read law at Lincoln's Springfield office. According to Lincoln biographer David Herbert Donald, the new president thought of him as "almost another son."

Dr. Holmes's Handiwork Dr. Thomas Holmes of New York offered to preserve Ellsworth's body free of charge, using his new fluid of bichloride of mercury—a safer and more effective alternative to ordinary embalming fluids. Viewing the colonel as he lay in state at the White House, the First Lady remarked that he looked "natural, as though he was sleeping a deep and peaceful sleep."

Holmes's handiwork brought him an army commission to embalm slain officers, and he would go on to prepare a reported 4,028 bodies for transport home and viewing. He and other embalmers were a godsend for families whose fallen soldiers could be sent home for burial looking much as they had in life.

☛ ABOUT AMPUTATIONS

It is no surprise that Civil War surgeons were called "sawbones," since the estimated 60,000 amputations performed accounted for more than three-quarters of all wartime operations. The blame lay mainly on the bullet called the minié ball, a single one of which could shatter several inches of bone.

The *Medical and Surgical History of the War of the Rebellion, 1861–1865* was a multivolume record compiled after the war by a team headed by Dr. Julian K. Barnes, the Union Army's second (and last) surgeon general. Part III, Volume II, tallied 29,980 amputations reported by Union and Confederate surgeons—by body part:

★ Hands and fingers: 7,970

★ Arms: 8,177

★ Legs: 12,153

★ Feet and toes: 1,680

Anesthetics Doctors and soldiers were unaware of germ theory and the antiseptics that would soon transform medicine. But thankfully, wounded soldiers could be anesthetized. Ether, used in hospitals up to the mid-twentieth century, induced deep sleep. Its alternative, chloroform, depressed the central nervous system. Opium and morphine were the most common pre-op and post-op painkillers.

☛ DR. MARY EDWARDS WALKER: Medical Pioneer

Mary Walker, born in upstate New York in 1832, followed in her physician father's footsteps and received her doctor's certificate. She would blaze more trails during the Civil War. As a civilian volunteer, she nursed wounded soldiers at battles from Bull Run to Chickamauga. Then, in the fall of 1863, the Army of the Cumberland commissioned her as an assistant surgeon—a first for a woman.

"Contrary Mary's" Attire Even Walker's clothing broke new ground. A champion of dress reform for women, "Contrary

Mary" (as she was called by many) often wore trousers, a man's black frock coat (in which she was both married and buried), and a top hat.

Later, when Walker was assistant surgeon for the 52nd Ohio Infantry, duty called her into enemy territory and she was arrested as a spy. Four months of imprisonment in Richmond surely marked another first for the determined doctor, as was the Medal of Honor she received in 1865 for her service First Bull Run.

Soft Hearts, Steel Nerves

Thousands of ordinary citizens dropped what they were doing to care for ailing Civil War soldiers. Others, including some famous names, were anything *but* ordinary.

☞ CLARA BARTON:
"Angel of the Battlefield"

Clara Barton

In April 1861 Clara Barton, a petite 39 year old who worked for the U.S. Patent Office in Washington, rushed to the Washington, D.C., railroad station to meet a battered regiment from her native Massachusetts. Given the dearth of medical supplies, the women she brought with her had to use their own handkerchiefs to dress the wounds of soldiers attacked in the Baltimore Riot (page 77). Shocked at how the troops lacked even basic necessities, Barton emptied her house of any useful items and delivered huge baskets of food she paid for herself.

A New Vocation From then on, Barton raised supplies for the Union Army and delivered them, often in the nick of time, to one makeshift hospital after another. She did what she could, holding soldiers' hands through the night or listening to them with compassion. After she bandaged injured soldiers at Antietam with the green leaves of corn stalks for want of bandages, one surgeon anointed her the "Angel of the Battlefield."

In 1870 Barton served with the International Red Cross in the Franco-Prussian War and, 11 years later, founded the American Red Cross.

☛ KATE CUMMING: Volunteer to Enlistee

Born in Scotland and raised in Mobile, Alabama, Kate Cumming bucked her parents' notion that battlefield nursing was inappropriate for young ladies and in April 1862 made her way to Shiloh, where close to 9,000 Confederate soldiers lay wounded. Then it was on to Chattanooga, where she enlisted in the Confederate Army Medical Department and began a nursing career that would last through the war.

Service in Tennessee and a number of field hospitals in Georgia led Cumming to record her day-to-day experiences, published in 1866 as *A Journal of Hospital Life in the Confederate Army of Tennessee*.

☛ MARY ANN BICKERDYKE: Woman on a Mission

Mary Ann Bickerdyke's take-charge attitude had already earned her the nickname "Mother Bickerdyke" in Galena, Illinois, whence she traveled downstate to a field hospital in Cairo. The 44-year-old widow—an herbalist by trade—had heard of the filthy conditions at the hospital.

By the time she left Cairo, the tents were orderly and clean, mattresses were stuffed with fresh straw, meals had gone from awful to taste-tempting and nutritious, and an army laundry was up and running. Bickerdyke had also found a calling, and by the war's end she had improved sanitation and living conditions for Union and Confederate soldiers alike. She was also beloved not only by the rank and file but by officers at the highest level, and gained national recognition as well.

☛ WALT WHITMAN: Male Nurse

When Walt Whitman, the poet who penned *Leaves of Grass,* spotted his brother George's name in a New York newspaper's list of the Fredericksburg wounded, he rushed to Maryland. George's injury turned out to be minor, but Whitman stayed for two weeks recording camp life in his journal and visiting injured soldiers.

When a Union Medical Department official asked Whitman to help the ailing to hospitals in Washington, he accepted the role. From then on he nursed convalescing soldiers almost daily, provided comfort and encouragement, and translated his experiences into poetry in *The Wound Dresser.*

☛ LOUISA MAY ALCOTT: Novelistic Nurse

The child of transcendentalist social reformers, Louisa May Alcott ran with the likes of Ralph Waldo Emerson and Henry David Thoreau. But her family circumstances—intellectually rich, monetarily poor—made her determined to make her own way. She began to write, and her first book was published in 1853, when she was 22.

Alcott was writing for *Atlantic Monthly* when the war began, and she enlisted as a nurse. Starting in 1862, she tended the sick at Washington's Union Hospital. And as writers do (see Walt Whitman), she published a book: *Hospital Sketches* (1863), based on candid letters she wrote home. *Little Women,* Alcott's contribution to the library of American classics, followed in 1868.

Soldiers at Their Leisure

Daily life in army camps during the 1860s was no picnic. The soldiers, separated from their families for months at a time, slept in uncomfortable tents, woke to the sound of reveille at 5 A.M., and (aside from gathering firewood, polishing guns, or marching in drills) spent vast stretches of time in unrelenting boredom. As one Mississippi volunteer put in 1864, "Oh how tiresome this camp life is to me...one everlasting monotone, yesterday, today, and tomorrow." The lulls were relieved, however, with the help of food, drink, and leisure-time distractions.

Near Petersburg, Virginia, soldiers of the 114th Pennsylvania Infantry look on as officers play cards.

Eats The army did not enlist experienced cooks, so the men took turns trying to transform their rations into edible meals. The results were mixed, but for the most part the fare was often unappetizing. In some companies the least competent soldiers were appointed cooks—their skills in the kitchen matching their skills on the battlefield. Union Army rations included pork, bacon, or beef (salt or fresh); beans or peas; rice or hominy; sugar, vinegar, and molasses. Confederate rations were much the same, though the meat was usually bacon and a soldier was lucky to come by a dried or fresh fruit or vegetable.

When the Union Army was on the move, rations consisted of salt pork and hardtack—unleavened biscuits also known as "tooth dullers," "sheet iron," or, if the hardtack was improperly stored and weevil-ridden, "worm castles." To soften it up, soldiers dunked hardtack in coffee or crumbled it into soup. Though hardtack wasn't unknown in the South, Confederate soldiers more often ate johnnycakes, cornmeal patties fried in bacon grease.

Drinks and Smokes Coffee energized soldiers and lifted their spirits; Southerners often had to caffeinate themselves with tea, since blockades of their ports made coffee rare. When fighting was in remission, coffee-rich Northerners and tobacco-rich Southerners sometimes traded these precious commodities.

Liquor was against the rules, but it was nevertheless consumed in large quantities. Alcoholic beverages took the form of either homemade moonshine (one chancy recipe called for bark juice, turpentine, and lamp oil), or store-bought whiskey smuggled into camp by those who welcomed a few hours of well-earned inebriation.

Games and Festivities Whenever possible, camp denizens played games: checkers, chess, cards, backgammon, dice, dominoes, horseshoes, and on occasion an early (and brutal) version of football. They also played baseball, a game especially popular in the North.

On holidays the camps took on an uncharacteristically festive air. The troops held boxing contests, horse races, and concerts. Popular songs of the time, whether plaintive tunes to soothe homesickness or rousing marching songs, were sung whenever a knot of soldiers felt the urge to raise their voices as well as their sagging spirits.

Critters Pets were forbidden but the more compassionate officers tended to look the other way. Dogs were the most common pets, and sometimes became mascots. The 11th Pennsylvania (the state's oldest volunteer regiment) kept a brindle bull terrier named Sallie—so beloved that her likeness lives on at the 11th Pennsylvania Monument at Gettysburg National Military Park.

THE
RECONSTRUCTION
ERA

1865–1877

Historians and Civil War buffs have long speculated on how Reconstruction—the readmitting of southern states into the Union—would have proceeded if President Abraham Lincoln had not been assassinated. A vastly more gifted politician than his successors Andrew Johnson and Ulysses S. Grant (in office from 1869 to 1877), Lincoln knew how to deliberate, compromise, and stand firm. As it was, Reconstruction began with legislative achievements that gave way to polarization, confrontation, fear, and continuing oppression.

Though the 11 states of the former Confederacy were technically under martial law, fewer than 30,000 Union soldiers were occupying the South by late 1866. Their remnants left for good in 1877, and the disenfranchisement of black Americans would last for decades on end.

Richmond lay in ruins on the eve of Reconstruction.

TWELVE FRUSTRATING YEARS

President Lincoln's tragic death coincided with the start of
Reconstruction. Subsequent brave attempts to "do the right thing"
did little to relieve the poor condition of the freed slaves, and the
federal government left Southerners wholly in charge in 1877.

―――≈⊙≈―――

A Fitful Start

Bumbling on the part of presidents Johnson and Grant, plus the
Radical Republicans' news-making hatred of the South, often
overshadowed men who were concerned first and foremost with
the interests of the freed slaves.

☛ FORD'S THEATER, April 16, 1865

When President Lincoln took his second oath of office on
March 4, 1865, the capitol dome rising above the crowd below
had been completed. The war still had not come to an end, and
Lincoln devoted his inaugural address to "the great contest
which still engrosses the energies of the nation."

A stone's throw away sat actor John Wilkes Booth, an actor
from one of America's first families of the stage and a die-hard
enemy of emancipation. Forty-nine days later he would use the
gun tucked in his pocket to shoot Lincoln at Ford's Theater. On
that night, as Abraham and Mary Lincoln sat chuckling over the
play *My American Cousin,* Booth burst into the box, fired at the
president's head, and then jumped to the stage and escaped.

The Missing Bodyguard Where, oh where, was a
bodyguard? No one is quite sure. John F. Parker, one of four
Washington policemen assigned to the security detail first created in November 1864, was supposed to be seated outside the

door to the box, but he is thought to have either gone downstairs to watch the play or to the Star Saloon next door.

The bigger question is why a man who had been repeatedly reprimanded for drunkenness and sleeping on the job was picked to protect the president. To add insult to injury, he wasn't fired until August 1868—for sleeping, not for his epic lapse at Ford's Theater.

☛ WHAT THE FREED DESIRED

Late in the war, President Lincoln had struggled with how to reunite the United States and what to do about the freed slaves. Though his Emancipation Proclamation was as political as humanitarian, the slaves in the South had taken freedom to heart, and their goals were not what most white people thought.

In January 1865 Secretary of War Edwin M. Stanton asked Gen. William T. Sherman to arrange a meeting with black leaders. Twenty guests, mostly ministers and the freeborn or freed, assembled at Sherman's headquarters in Savannah, Georgia. The discussion, now known as the Savannah Colloquy, was calm, serious, and, as Stanton had stipulated, "intelligent."

Self Reliance Asked what freed slaves expected of freedom, the group's spokesman, Baptist minister Garrison Frazier, replied, "Placing us where we could reap the fruit of our own labor and take care of ourselves." The black men spoke of enough land to support their families, the full rights of citizenship, and being left alone to enjoy the promises of freedom as they saw fit.

☛ "SHERMAN LAND"

With Lincoln's approval, General Sherman issued Special Field Order No. 15 four days after the Savannah meeting: Some 400,000 acres of rich, coastal plantation land were to be divided into 40-acre plots for the exclusive use of free blacks.

Distributing this land, confiscated after white owners fled, solved one of the general's biggest headaches: thousands of former slaves who had attached themselves to his military force for protection. Sherman apparently intended his order as a temporary expedient, but for the freedmen, "Sherman Land" offered a permanent home.

Back to Square One Sherman Land came to a quick and inglorious end. First, President Johnson rescinded Order No. 15. Then, as planters regained their plantations under Johnson's pardons plan, Congress overwhelmingly rejected efforts to make what Thaddeus Stevens called the "forfeited estates of the enemy" available to freedmen. Most black farmers had no choice: They became poorly paid contract laborers on the land where they had recently been slaves.

☛ ANDREW JOHNSON: Wrong Man for the Job

When Vice President Andrew Johnson succeeded Abraham Lincoln, the country had reason to be hopeful. Born into extreme poverty, illiterate until his twenties (his wife taught him to read and write), and a natural populist politician, Johnson personified an American ideal: the hardscrabble, bootstrapping self-made man. This "accidental" president from Tennessee also had an impressive résumé—successful businessman, state legislator and governor, member of the U.S. House and Senate—plus fierce loyalty to the Union and Lincoln's Reconstruction goals. But Johnson was no Lincoln.

Obstinacy and Spite An egotistical and self-righteous loner, Johnson seldom took advice and was immune to persuasion, incapable of compromise, and devoid of tact. His gift for spiteful, incendiary rhetoric secured his career as a "man of the people" in up-country Appalachia but failed him in the wider world. Negative reactions to his vicious personal attacks

Good Laws and Bad

A flurry of legislation reflected a nation still mired in conflict. It began with "freedom amendments" to the U.S. Constitution and ended two decades after Reconstruction with a Dred Scott-style court decision.

Thirteenth Amendment (ratified December 18, 1865) Abolished all forms of slavery and involuntary servitude, except as punishment for convicted criminals.

Military Reconstruction Acts Four laws enacted in 1867 and 1868 to establish and define military supervision of Reconstruction.

Fourteenth Amendment (ratified July 28, 1868) Defined citizenship for all born and naturalized persons; guaranteed rights to jury trials, full protection of the law, and due process.

Fifteenth Amendment (ratified March 30, 1870) Guaranteed right to vote regardless of "race, color, or previous condition of servitude."

Enforcement Acts Three laws, passed in May 1870 and February and April 1871 and also known as Civil Rights Acts, enabled the federal government to prosecute voter intimidation cases and rein in the Ku Klux Klan and other domestic terrorist groups in the South.

Civil Rights Act of 1875 Guaranteed "full and equal access" to public conveyances, inns, theaters, and places of amusement; established right to serve on juries regardless of race. Though later gutted by the Supreme Court, this is regarded as the country's first public accommodations act.

***Plessy vs. Ferguson* Decision** (May 18, 1896) Upheld a Louisiana law mandating separate but equal accommodations on intrastate railroads and led to other state laws segregating whites and blacks.

on Radical Republicans during the 1865 presidential campaign strengthened the power of these political enemies in Congress—and the result would be a stalemate of monstrous proportions.

☛ THE OTHER SIDE: RADICAL REPUBLICANS

Committed to absolute equality for all black people and extended punishment for the white South, the radical wing of the Republican Party had initially thought President Johnson was of like mind. But his unilateral actions during Congress's lengthy 1865 recess told them otherwise. So the radicals, led by senators Stevens of Pennsylvania and Sumner of Massachusetts, decided that Congress *must* take charge.

Thaddeus the Terrible Thaddeus Stevens, whose poor childhood mirrored Johnson's, was an outspoken abolitionist. He had orchestrated slave escapes via the Underground Railroad, helped found the antislavery Republican Party, and welcomed the Civil War as the final blow against the despised South. (The feeling was mutual. When Lee's army invaded Pennsylvania, Confederates deliberately destroyed an ironworks owned by Stevens. Jubal Early vowed to hang the Yankee senator, then display his bones as "curiosities.") No one was safe from Stevens's oratorical invective, so brilliantly hateful that his harangues ultimately alienated his own party.

Charles the Cursed Charles Sumner was a child of privilege, a Harvard Law graduate, and a pacifist abolitionist who first made his name in 1845 by presenting an antiwar lecture to an audience of military veterans. In 1854 he shocked the senate by delivering "The Crime Against Kansas"—a diatribe in which he labeled fellow senator Andrew Butler as South Carolina's Don Quixote serving "the harlot Slavery." A few days later Sumner was mercilessly beaten by a cane-wielding nephew of Butler's, and it took him three years to recover.

☛ IMPEACHMENT AND RADICAL OVERREACH

If Johnson was an "immovable object," Congress was the "irresistible force." Guided by the Radicals, Congress passed law after law to control Reconstruction. Johnson struck back with vetoes, and for the first time in American history, Congress retaliated by excising its override power. Meanwhile, Radical Republicans sought grounds to rid themselves of the president. A new law—the Tenure of Office Act guaranteeing that federal officials appointed with senate approval could not be removed without senate approval—became the weapon.

The Attempt When Johnson fired Secretary of War Edwin M. Stanton without consulting Congress, he intended to test the constitutionality of the Tenure law in court, but in 1868 the Radicals responded with impeachment. Eleven charges, eight related to Tenure, were passed by the House with no discussion.

> If Johnson was an "immovable object,"
> Congess was the "irresistible" force.

The Outcome While the Radicals ranted, Johnson's legal team demolished each charge. Seven moderate Republicans defected to vote against conviction, leaving the senate one vote short of a two-thirds majority.

Johnson won, but the trial destroyed his slim hope for another term. The Radicals' loss accelerated their fading influence. Object and force had collided, and both imploded.

☛ THE FREEDMAN'S BUREAU

The Freedman's Bureau was arguably the best idea anyone had in the Reconstruction era—and was thereby doomed from the start. Functioning under military control and directed by Oliver O. Howard, the officially named Bureau of Refugees, Freed-

In Alfred R. Waud's drawing The Freedman's Bureau *(1868), a bureau agent tries to keep the peace between white and freed slaves.*

men, and Abandoned Lands acted with the best intentions to prepare and equip freed slaves for life in a postwar society.

Hope or Failure? Congress initially empowered the Bureau to set aside confiscated and abandoned lands for black and white heads of households to rent or purchase. Renewed in 1866, the authorization was extended for two more years and expanded to include educational functions and guarantee certain civil rights, including "equal protection" with military assistance, if needed.

In 1868 Congress gave the Bureau another year to finish its work but allowed its education programs to continue indefinitely. The doors closed on January 1, 1868 (though Howard remained), and the education efforts ended during the economic crisis of 1873.

☛ OLIVER O. HOWARD: Bureau Head, Educator

Maine-born and West Point–trained Oliver Otis Howard was nicknamed "the Christian general" for his strict adherence to biblical principles, even in battle. Howard endured a string of setbacks in the Civil War, including the loss of his right arm, then redeemed himself magnificently at the Battle of Chattanooga and earned General Sherman's respect during the March to the Sea.

Howard's postwar reward was to head the new Freedmen's Bureau—a thankless task in the poisonous climate of Reconstruction. Historians generally agree, however, that no one was better suited for the task than this honest, able man who was willing to buck allies as well as enemies. (When he refused to make the bureau into a political arm of the Republican Party, he was falsely accused of gross mismanagement in a failed effort to oust him.)

Howard University Howard realized that integrating freed slaves into the culture would be a lengthy process and his job was to lay a firm foundation. His commitment included the creation of a number of schools and colleges, most notably Howard University, future cradle of the mid-twentieth century's civil rights movement.

"Nobody Knows the Trouble I've Seen"

If Abraham Lincoln's eyes welled with tears as he listened to fugitive slaves sing spirituals in 1863 (page 122), he would have surely wept bitter tears over the concerted postwar efforts to keep blacks oppressed.

☛ THE SOUTH'S BLACK CODES

The so-called Black Codes that began to be enacted by southern states and localities in 1866 generally granted limited freedoms to blacks—to marry, sign contracts, sue and be sued, and testify in court against other blacks (but not whites). Other codes

Four Abolitionists Postwar

Key abolitionists from the antebellum years lived to see the slaves freed and positive laws enacted. But what became of Douglass, Garrison, Phillips, and Smith?

Frederick Douglass Douglass was close to Susan B. Anthony and Elizabeth Cady Stanton—both activist abolitionists in their youth—and spoke at the Seneca Falls woman's suffrage convention. But their friendship faltered as the Fifteenth Amendment made its way through Congress and Stanton and Anthony lobbied for the act to include women. Douglass believed black men took precedence and that woman's suffrage would naturally follow.

The dispute dissolved when Douglass fought for women's rights after the Fifteenth Amdendment's ratification. Douglass died in February 1895 after attending a meeting of the Women's National Council in Washington, D.C.

William Lloyd Garrison, Wendell Phillips With the slaves free, William Lloyd Garrison wanted to shut down *The Liberator* and the American Slavery Society, feeling a "mission accomplished" statement was preferable to entering the foreboding forest of Reconstruction. Wendell Phillips begged to differ and took over editorship of the newspaper and kept the society running until 1870. Both men continued to work for social reform until their deaths in 1879 and 1884.

Gerrit Smith In 1867 the Chicago *Tribune* reported that Gerrit Smith had feigned insanity to escape prosecution for helping fund John Brown's raid at Harpers Ferry. Smith sued for libel, but the court ruled against him. The same year, Smith joined with Horace Greeley and Cornelius Vanderbilt to underwrite the million-dollar bond required to free the unrepentant Jefferson Davis, jailed for almost two years even though he had not been charged with any crime.

denied blacks firearms, educational opportunities equal to those of whites, and unimpeded access to the ballot box.

(No) Right to Work The most damaging codes coerced and controlled black labor. Using a self-serving interpretation of vagrancy, states required blacks to show proof of employment to avoid arrest and fines. Proof meant signed labor contracts, usually with the newly restored plantation owners. To keep wages low, employers were prohibited from "enticing" black contract workers with offers of higher pay or better conditions. "Apprenticeship" laws allowed government officials to seize black children from their families and hand them over to white "guardians," who put them to work without pay.

Codes Gone, Pattern Set Black Codes were built on a gaping legal loophole: Lincoln emancipated the slaves but hadn't made them citizens. Though the Black Codes collapsed with ratification of the Fourteenth Amendment in 1868, they set patterns of "second-class" citizenship that persisted for generations.

Carpetbaggers and Scalawags

Even now the Reconstruction terms "carpetbagger" and "scalawag" carry the odor of corruption and opportunism. But they weren't always so negative. "Carpetbaggers" originally applied to people who came South after the war and participated in politics, civil service, and business ventures; the word traces to the tapestry travel valises they often carried. The source of "scalawag"—any Southerner who sided with the Union in the war and supported its Reconstruction efforts—is unclear.

There is no real evidence that carpetbaggers and scalawags—almost all white and Republican—were better or worse than the rest of America. Yet as the historically addled mythology of the Lost Cause took hold (pages 168–169), carpetbaggers and scalawags were transformed into vicious stereotypes: cunning con artists, evil tyrants, race traitors, and enemies of the Cause.

☛ RISE AND FALL OF THE KKK

Started in December 1865 as a kind of frat-boy prank by a half-dozen bored young men in rural Pulaski, Tennessee, the Ku Klux Klan fired the imaginations of Southerners with anything but benign intentions. Scholars have speculated how it spread; possibly the costumes, secret rituals, arcane titles, and inexplicable name gave credence to gangs of whites who prowled the night.

Though brutal attacks on freed blacks and white scalawags predated the KKK, new Klans and similar paramilitary groups sprang up across the South—independent terrorist cells threatening, beating, whipping, raping, and murdering at will. Victims were mainly black men, but black women and children and whites regarded as race traitors were vulnerable, too.

Forrest Bows Out The Klan was chartered in 1867 with Nathan Bedford Forrest as its "Grand Dragon." Forrest later tried to disband the organization, to little effect. Prosecutions were nearly impossible. Local law enforcement was often Klan controlled, and few dared to testify against them.

Enforcement of civil rights laws in the early 1870s put a dent in the "Invisible Empire," but only with the late '70s return of segregation-friendly governments did the Invisible Empire begin to fade away.

☛ GRANT IN THE WHITE HOUSE

Tired of the rancorous standoff between President Johnson and the radicals in Congress, Americans turned in 1868 to their hero, Gen. Ulysses S. Grant. He seemed the right choice for the Republicans—a great leader in war, committed to a speedy reunification of the states, and respected across political lines. Winning the electoral college by a landslide, Grant supported Congress's tough approach to Reconstruction. One of his major achievements was the use of federal troops to enforce the

Ku Klux Klan Act of 1871, one of the two Enforcement Acts of that year (page 155).

A Second-Term Challenge Grant was increasingly engulfed in financial turmoil, and Reconstruction often took a back seat. He also found himself challenged by a splinter party: the Liberal Republicans (a misnomer in modern terms) who opposed continuation of his Reconstruction policies, supported Southern self rule, and sought to shift the public focus to industry and expansion. In alliance with Democrats, the Liberal Republicans nominated Horace Greeley for president in 1872. Grant won, thanks in no small measure to black voters in the South.

> **Following the Wall Street crash of 1873, the country fell into a severe depression...**

Lost in the Crash Following the Wall Street crash of 1873, the country fell into a severe depression, accompanied by a wave of high-level bribery and corporate corruption scandals unparalleled in American history. Blameless himself, Grant seemed deliberately blind to the revelations. Loyal to a fault, he trusted the people around him long after their crimes were exposed.

Though often cited as one of the weakest American presidents, Grant nevertheless oversaw the ratification of the Fifteenth Amendment and passage of the Civil Rights Act of 1875. But he never understood the difference between politics and friendship. He not only lost his bid for a third term but was left bankrupt by Wall Street fraudsters.

☛ ADELBERT AMES: Misunderstood Carpetbagger

In 1861 Maine native Adelbert Ames went straight from his West Point graduation to war and within two months had proved his mettle. Severely wounded during First Bull Run, the 26-year-old officer refused to leave the field, an act acknowledged with a Medal of Honor. Ames recovered and continued to serve with distinction, but his biggest battles lay ahead.

It began with Ames's 1868 military appointment as provisional governor of Mississippi, replacing Benjamin Humphreys. Ames's first unpleasant duty was the physical removal of Humphreys, a former Confederate brigadier general, from the governor's mansion. Mississippi's Republican legislature sent Ames to the U.S. Senate in 1870, and he was elected governor in 1873.

Old Planters Prevail Ames pushed hard for reform, especially the expansion of civil rights for freed slaves. But as the old planter class grew more powerful, factional violence escalated. President Grant refused Ames's appeals for federal intervention, so under threat of impeachment, he resigned in 1876. He became a successful Massachusetts businessman, returning once to active duty as a fighting general in the Spanish-American War.

Reputation Repaired? A man of integrity and intelligence, Ames was the antithesis of the mythical Yankee carpetbagger—but old myths die hard. After the 1956 publication of *Profiles in Courage,* Ames's daughter fought to correct the misrepresentation of her father's Mississippi years in John F. Kennedy's popular book. Though the book went uncorrected, historians have since restored the maligned carpetbagger's good name.

☞ BLACK MEN ENTER GOVERNMENT

When Hiram Rhodes Revels, a well-educated minister and Civil War veteran, walked into the U.S. Senate chamber in February 1870 and took the oath of office, it was a groundbreaking moment. Revels was the first black American senator, elected by Mississippi's Reconstruction legislature after a bitter contest with the state's Conservative Democrats. Revels served only a year but was soon followed by Senator Blanche Kelso Bruce, also from Mississippi, and 16 African-American Republicans elected to the House.

Hardworking Symbols Most of these men worked diligently rather than spectacularly, largely because white Republicans valued them more as symbols of Reconstruction than as colleagues. A similar pattern developed in local and state elections throughout the South. Black officeholders were marginalized by white Republican leaders and denied any real political power.

☛ THE COLFAX MASSACRE

The bloodiest race crime of Reconstruction occurred on April 13, 1873, in Louisiana. Though the Ku Klux Klan was in decline, the supremacist White League remained strong in the state. League men had no need to hide behind bed sheets and ride by night, and they openly targeted Republicans.

Reacting to the contentious gubernatorial contest that put Republican William Kellogg in office, the League laid siege to the Republican government in Colfax, seat of the largely black Grant parish. In anticipation, the townspeople armed themselves and fortified the courthouse, holding it safe for three weeks—but a messenger carrying a request for help to the governor was waylaid.

Attack on Easter Sunday As Easter dawned, the white "militia men"—with guns, a small cannon, and KKK reinforcements—gave women and children 30 minutes to leave the courthouse grounds. Then they attacked. Details are disputed, but as the defenders raised white flags, a League man was shot, and the slaughter began. In the end, three white men and dozens of blacks (estimates range from 80 to 150) died. Many defenders were murdered while fleeing or being held prisoner.

Laura Towne: Woman of Good Deeds

Kept illiterate by force, freed slaves understood the power of education. Their first teachers were black men who, though rarely well educated, could read and write. Then white teachers, about 80 percent of them idealistic women sponsored by Northern benevolent societies, began arriving. Threatened by local whites, many returned home disillusioned. But not Pittsburg-born Laura Towne, a trained homeopathic physician.

The Port Royal Experiment Towne joined the 1862 Port Royal Experiment, a venture in black self-governance under the Union army in the Sea Islands of South Carolina. The experiment fell apart when former white owners reclaimed the islands. But Towne stayed on, helping to found the Penn School on St. Helena's Island. The school's demanding curriculum trained future black teachers and leaders.After Towne's death in 1901, the focus shifted to technical training. Closed in 1948, Penn became a community services center and was a training site for Martin Luther King's Southern Christian Leadership Conference in the 1960s.

★ ★ ★ ★ ★ ★ ★ ★ ★ ★ ★ THE CELEBRATED ★ ★ ★ ★ ★ ★ ★ ★ ★ ★ ★

Justice Denied Despite the courageous fight of U.S. Attorney J. R. Beckwith to prosecute the League under federal jurisdiction, only nine were tried. After two trials, three men were convicted of conspiracy and lesser crimes, but the convictions were voided by a Supreme Court justice.

☛ THE LAST CONFEDERATE

After his capture on May 10, 1865, Jefferson Davis was imprisoned at Fort Monroe, Virginia, for two years while everyone argued about his fate. Indicted for treason, the president of the defunct Confederacy was finally released on bail though never brought to trial.

No Remorse Under President Johnson's lenient amnesty and pardons policy, Davis could have petitioned for restoration of his citizenship. But unlike other high-ranking Confederates, he maintained that secession had been legal under the U.S. Constitution and steadfastly refused to take the required loyalty oath or apologize to anyone.

Davis's two-volume *The Rise and Fall of the Confederacy* (1881) was well received in the South, sparkling a revival of his popularity and new vigor to defend the Lost Cause (pages 168–169).Davis died in 1889, still unrepentant and unreconstructed—a man without a country.

☛ ELECTION OF 1876 = End of an Era

Until the Bush–Gore contest of 2000, Americans hadn't experienced a presidential election as tangled as 1876, when Democrat Samuel Tilden of New York handily beat Republican Rutherford B. Hayes in the popular vote but lost the race. It came down to a handful of disputed votes in the electoral college. Tilden needed just one more vote, and Hayes was down by 20. After weeks of wrangling and efforts by both parties to buy votes, the Republicans cut a deal with Southern Democrats, and Hayes won the prize.

Both Hayes and Tilden had pledged to end Reconstruction. Once in office, Hayes (nicknamed "Rutherfraud" by the eastern press) promptly fulfilled his promise.

Federal Troops Withdraw In April 1877 the last federal troops in the South were withdrawn from Louisiana and South Carolina, dropping the final barrier to the Conservative Democrats' takeover of the Southern state governments.

The dwindling antebellum aristocracy and a new breed of southern politicians determined to "modernize" the South for profit joined hands. And they were now free to take back the gains made under Reconstruction, including measures that subjected blacks to "slavery by another name" (page 169).

The Aftermath

Reconstruction illuminated the depths of racism in every corner of American society. Only a few whites could grasp the realities facing four million men, women, and children suddenly freed after two centuries of inherited bondage. Even good-hearted whites grew weary of "the Negro problem," while others blamed blacks for the war's tumultuous aftermath.

The Freedman's Bureau (page 157), the most potentially productive of all Reconstruction efforts, was killed off just as it was making some headway—and the notion that helping blacks would make them "dependent" took hold.

In the South, freedmen with voting rights and loyalty to the party of Lincoln were threatening to the Conservative Democrat elites. Reconstruction led directly to disenfranchisement of black voters with Jim Crow laws (named after a minstrel character who originated in the 1840s) and "separate but equal" segregation enshrined in the Supreme Court's 1896 *Plessy vs Ferguson* decision (page 155). *Plessy* remained in place until *Brown vs Board of Education* was decided in 1954.

"Slavery By Another Name" Slave labor had been essential to the Old South (and national) economy. After the war, the South accepted that freed blacks should be paid for their work but used every maneuver imaginable to keep them landless and at the bottom of the economic heap, resulting in systemic impoverishment and "slavery by another name."

Southern power wielders also managed to drive a permanent wedge between former slaves and working-class whites, especially in up-country regions where slavery had never taken hold. What is now referred to as "going against one's own best interests" in politics reflects this manufactured antagonism.

The "Lost Cause" Movement The Lost Cause movement, adopted by the so-called Dunning School of scholars at the turn of the twentieth century, cast secession as a principled defense of states' rights unrelated to slavery. It also posed the Confederacy as a valiant failure wrought by internal betrayals. Closely related was "Old South" nostalgia that romanticized the antebellum South of the planter class as mostly benign, except for the occasional wicked Yankee overseer. These rewritings of history spawned countless novels, and films and survived into the television era. Director D. W. Griffith lauded the Ku Klux Klan in the racist silent film *Birth of a Nation* (1915), which not only had its premiere at President Woodrow Wilson's White House but also garnered the highest box-office grosses of the silent era. Margaret Mitchell's novel *Gone With the Wind* (1936) painted a more realistic picture of the Old South, but the classic 1939 film bolstered Lost Cause mythology.

Positive Blowback If Reconstruction imploded, it also affirmed the freed slaves' faith in education, which they doggedly pursued with little outside assistance; the lawyers who overturned "separate but equal" and college students who spearheaded the civil rights movement of the 1950s and '60s were their legacy. In addition, the rampant corruption of the era raised public awareness of business-political conniving and opened the way for labor reforms and financial regulation. And women leveraged the Fourteenth Amendment to gain universal suffrage.

So how to evaluate Reconstruction? As novelist Charles Dickens—a native son of

"Worse Than Slavery," reads the plaque flanked by a White Leaguer and a Klansman.

the then not-so-distant mother country—wrote in another context, "It was the spring of hope, it was the winter of despair...."

Index

Note: Page numbers in *italic* refer to illustrations or photographs.

About the Author

Fred DuBose, a native Texan, is a writer, editor, and book developer based in New York City. He is an author of *Oh, Say Did You Know,* as well as an eclectic collection of books with subjects as varied as tomatoes, grandparents, cooking, and wine.

The Classics

From the Acropolis and Homer's *Odyssey* to "carpe diem" and Zeus. This book contains all the stuff you'd ever want to know about classical literature, language, philosophy, art, math, and more—without any of the stuffiness.

Caroline Taggart

ISBN 978-1-60652-132-8

Spilling the Beans on the Cat's Pajamas

This book spills the beans on our best-loved euphemisms and most curious sayings, explaining their fascinating origins and the remarkable stories that surround them. It rounds up the usual suspects—the hundreds of catch phrases and expressions that enrich our everyday speech and makes them easy to find in an A-to-Z format.

Judy Parkinson

ISBN 978-1-60652-171-7

An Apple a Day

Discover the origins and meanings of proverbs—those colorful, time-honored truths that enrich our language and culture. You'll learn why these sayings have stood the test of time.

Caroline Taggart

ISBN 978-1-60652-191-5

DON'T FORGET THESE BESTSELLERS
A Certain "Je Ne Sais Quoi"
Easy as Pi
E=MC²

Each Book is $14.95 hardcover

For more information visit us at RDTradePublishing.com

E-book editions also available.

Reader's Digest books can be purchased through retail and online bookstores. In the United States books are distributed by Penguin Group (USA), Inc. For more information or to order books, call 1-800-788-6262.